L.L. Bean

Fly-Casting Handbook

L.L. Bean
Fly-Casting
Handbook

MACAULEY LORD

PHOTOGRAPHS BY
JIM ROWINSKI

The Lyons Press

To my brother, Sam,
and to the memory of that day on Yellowstone Lake
when He guided us.

First Edition

Printed in Canada

Designed by Compset, Inc.

10 9 8 7 6 5 4 3 2 1

Library of Congress Cataloging-in-Publication Data

Lord, Macauley.
    L.L. Bean fly-casting handbook/Macauley Lord; photography by
        Jim Rowinski.
        p.   cm.
    ISBN 1-55821-964-1 (pb)
    1. Fly casting—Handbooks, manuals, etc.   I. Title

SH454.2.L67   1999
799.1´24—dc21   99-051997

Contents

Preface

Any fish worth catching is worth catching well. That's what draws us to fly fishing. We use the tiniest, most delicate lures imaginable. Many are little more than pieces of fine fluff. We cast them with one of the most graceful motions found in all of sport. And we fight most of our fish in a starkly primitive manner, by holding onto the line and manually pulling the fish to us. But flies and fighting fish are for other books: this one is about that graceful motion, the cast, fly fishing's poem.

There are few things as beautiful as casting a fly. When done properly, a cast can be sublime—simple physics translated into aerial ballet. On the greatest days, we forget that we are even using a fly rod; we look at a place on the water and our fly just seems to land there. There are also times, usually when the fishing is slow and our minds are wandering, when the rod takes over, demanding our full attention. It becomes almost a magic wand, one that we cast and cast, trying to make that one perfect cast. Just for the joy of it. Just to see that loop of line unfurl in the sky above our heads. Just so, on the way home from the water, we might think, "I made some great casts today. The loops had symmetry, but the bottom had a tiny bounce in it. Maybe next time I can throw a cast that's even better."

I wrote this book to take you closer to the perfect cast, the cast that seems to make itself while you stand by and watch in awe. Physicists speak of an elegant theory, one that is precise, neat, simple. That is what I hope for your casting: that, though falling short of perfection, it may be precise, neat, and simple, without excess motion. The elegant cast is the simple cast, the one that quiets the body and the mind, making room for reverence of fishes and waters.

These pages reflect my bias as a fly-fishing generalist. Few self-respecting trout specialists would teach the double haul before the reach cast. But the double haul is more fun and, unlike the reach, is used in the pursuit of nearly all types of fish.

Whether this is your first day or twentieth year of fly fishing, the methods in these pages will help you become a better caster. They are based on two decades of collective casting wisdom refined at the L.L. Bean Fly-Fishing School, and on the teaching of the leading casting instructors of our time. You'll learn how to make a simple four-part cast and to progress step-by-step through roll casting, false casting, shooting, and coping with wind. You'll learn advanced techniques such as double hauling and slack-line casts. You'll learn why heavy flies require imperfect, almost ugly, casts. You'll also learn some

tricks that will help you when things go wrong. Along the way, there are strange offerings such as the belly cast and the inverted reel cast. We'll kick a few dogmas, too: like the ones that say you are supposed to watch your backcast, wait for the tug at the end of the backcast, and land the fly before the line.

The truth is that absolute perfection in casting is unattainable. But think of all the fun you'll have trying! One day in 1978, I was fishing Slough Creek in Yellowstone National Park when the fish were practically begging me to put my grasshopper imitation on the water. Instead, I put the fly in the tall grass behind me—dozens of times, it seemed, under a hot sun and hounded by mosquitoes. It was driving me crazy to have to repeatedly unhook my fly from that grass. I was a *long* way from perfection in those days.

Back home, I replaced my fiberglass rod with a longer, stiffer graphite model and I practiced making more vertical backcast stops. By the time I was able to take another trip to Yellowstone, my casting was much improved. Fishing that stream the second time was like a dream from which I have never awakened. All day long, I put the fly on the water and all day long the fish ate it. I've since caught more fish and bigger fish in one day, but that was my first day of trout fishing heaven. The memory inspires me to this day.

Whether you are practicing on your lawn or fishing the water of your dreams, you will always have the luxury of making the elegant cast. But there will be many times when you are unhappy with your results. I've been there countless times; I'm always amused when I make a casting mistake at the Fly-Fishing School, and the students think that I did it on purpose.

You will find that your casting errors diminish over time. Your loops will become streamlined, the line above will seem to float, your rod will not even whisper during the backcast, and the fly will land out where the fish are. You'll notice that the fish will come easier. You'll get that sound in your voice, that lift in your spirit that I've heard and seen in so many of my L.L. Bean casting students when they say, "This is *great!*"

I admit that I have cast for hours on end over dewy lawns and fishless waters. I've been enthralled by that feeling of casting well, that quality of motion that I want to teach you. Like me, you may discover that you can wander out into the backyard and be hypnotized watching that loop of line leap from your rod tip as you false cast into the air, where large fish levitate in your imagination and the fishing never ends.

While I've never made that perfect cast, I'm still trying.

Acknowledgments

A teacher learns mostly from others, some from his own experience, and passes the knowledge on. Those from whom I've learned include some of the great names in casting: Jim Green, the dean of West Coast casting instructors, whose 1975 film, "Secrets of Fly Casting," taught me how to accelerate the rod and whose confidence in me as a casting instructor changed my life; Mel Krieger, fly casting's poet, whose vision to raise the standards for casting instruction came to fruition in the Federation of Fly Fishers' Casting Instructor Certification Program. Mel's book, *The Essence of Fly Casting,* set the standard for all casting books to come. I have also been fortunate to learn from Joan Wulff, an extraordinarily innovative and graceful mentor to casters for more than half a century, who continues to share her visionary teaching methods with us; Lefty Kreh, whose wonderful style with a fly rod and sincere affection for all fly fishers has made him the Pied Piper of our sport; and Gary Borger, who helped me control my backcast in West Yellowstone in 1981 and whose books, articles, and videos have raised the bar for fly fishers and their teachers everywhere. All of my teachers and mentors may find things in this book with which they disagree, perhaps passionately. May they understand. . . .

No teacher could have a better education than my twelve years of casting colloquy with the gifted instructors of the L.L. Bean Fly-Fishing School. They have included Dave Whitlock, Joe Robinson, John Kluesing, Dave Hagengruber, John Sharkey, Ellen Peters, Brian Golden, and Joe Codd. To hear us discuss casting, you'd have thought we were trying to agree on a rewrite of the

Ten Commandments. During those times, it was often Pat Jackson who cheer-fully reminded us that we were only talking about fly casting.

Joe Codd provided early comments on the tone of this book. It is better for his suggestions. Dana Dodge provided a punch line, perhaps the only one. Steve Meyers, author, guide, and friend of rivers, was invaluable during our photo-shoot in Colorado. If only he could have kept it from snowing every day.

Known to the pros as the best unheralded casting instructor on the conti-nent, Bruce Richards of Scientific Anglers provided fly lines that photograph and cast beautifully. Rich Best of G.Loomis provided the great white rod. Bill Gammel, his father's greatest student, told me the story of Jay Gammel's last cast. Captain Brock Apfel guided me over many new waters. When an injury kept me from casting, Kyle Whyet prayed for me, and my wife, Carol, wouldn't let me fall.

Jim Rowinski proposed this book and asked me to write it. He's also the one who brought me to the L.L. Bean Fly-Fishing School many years ago. If it weren't for Jim, I might have a real job.

Introduction:
How to Use This Book

If you are new to fly fishing, read the chapters in order. You'll get an approximation of what a student at the L.L. Bean Fly-Fishing School learns, but without the hands-on help. When you stumble, reread the descriptions of the steps you are learning. And remember that mistakes are one of your best teachers: to learn to cast is often to learn how *not* to cast. If reviewing the steps doesn't fix the problem, go to the "Troubleshooting" section at the end of the chapter.

The shaded boxes in each chapter contain some casting wisdom, some fish stories, and some tangents. Most will deepen your understanding of the cast. The boxes at the beginning of each chapter will provide you with a context for what you are about to learn.

Take this book outside with you and study the photographs. Mimic them. Move your hand, arm, and rod into the positions you see in the book. This book assumes that you are right-handed. For example, when the book talks about forming a "D" during the roll cast, a left-hander will need to mentally reverse this analogy. Make sure that you understand each photograph and the text that accompanies it before moving ahead.

Other than a casting instructor, the most valuable companion to this book is a video camera. Using the pause button, freeze the tape of your casting at the various stop positions to make sure you are making the casting motions as shown in the illustrations. (There's more about how to videotape yourself in Chapter 6.)

Even if you have been casting for a long time, you'll find some pearls in these pages. Students at the L.L. Bean School who come to us with years of experience marvel at how much there is still to learn, even about something such as a 45-foot cast that they may have taken for granted. If you just want to learn to cast farther, or with more ease, *check your fundamentals first.* Review Chapter 2, "The Four-Part Cast on a Lawn." Practice the pop/stop with your elbow close to your body, relaxed at your side. Try the casts at the end of that chapter in the **Playing Around** section. Then go to Chapter 5 on "False Casting" and do the drills listed under **Tip Casting, Midsection Casting,** and **Playing Around.** Then go to Chapter 6, "Lengthening Your Cast," and study the section on **Shooting Beyond 45 Feet.** Be sure to try the **Playing Around** drills in that chapter. Then go on to Chapter 8, "The Double Haul," and Chapter 9, "Special Casts."

You have set a high bar for yourself: learning to cast from a book is harder than learning from a live instructor. If you like what you read here and you want to learn more, attend the L.L. Bean Fly-Fishing School (1–800-FISH-LLB) or one of the other good casting programs around the country. Another option is to contact the Federation of Fly Fishers (FFF) in Bozeman, Montana, at 406/585–7592. As the governing body for casting instructors in the United States and Canada, they will gladly refer you to an FFF-Certified Casting Instructor or Master Casting Instructor in your area.

Eleven Habits of Highly Effective Casters

For skilled casters, most of the following are truly habitual, things they do without question. For example, they practice and often fish with a bright line so they can see what the line is doing. They use a small practice fly to keep it from dominating the line and leader. They clean the line so it shoots well. They wear a hat and sunglasses.

Get into the habit of doing these things and they will become second nature for you, too. You'll be happy if you do. Your casting and fishing will suffer if you don't.

USE THE RIGHT OUTFIT

An ideal outfit for many beginners to learn and fish with is an 8½- or 9-foot graphite rod designed for a 5- or 6-weight line. Few fly rodders are without a rod in this size and weight range. Most trout guides will tell you that they could spend their lifetimes happily fishing with one of these rods.

Grandpa's old bamboo rod should be kept on the mantlepiece. Bamboo rods are beautiful anachronisms: They're aesthetically superior but functionally inferior to graphite rods. To a lesser degree, the same is true of fiberglass rods: There are some pleasant-casting fiberglass rods, but a good graphite rod makes casting easier than a good fiberglass rod. When you are first learning, even if you are learning an advanced skill like the double haul, you owe it to yourself to have every advantage.

An outfit is properly matched when the line weight matches the line designation on the rod, and the reel is of the appropriate size to hold the

What Is a 6-Weight Line?

Fly lines are grouped according to how much they weigh in the front 30 feet, the part closest to the leader and tippet. A 6-weight line is slightly heavier than a 5-weight line and therefore requires a rod that is a tad stouter than a 5-weight rod needs to be. A 12-weight line is extremely heavy, requires a very stiff rod, and is used to cast heavy flies to huge fish. A 3-weight line is very light, requires a delicate rod, and is used to cast very small flies.

correct line. If you are not sure whether your outfit is matched, call the L.L. Bean Fly-Fishing experts (1–800-FISH-LLB) to ask their opinion, or take your outfit to a fly-fishing specialty shop. As a general rule, buy your tackle from one of the firms that specializes in fly fishing. This is a complex sport, and an uninformed clerk or inappropriate purchase can make fly fishing too difficult.

If you are a small person, or if you think you may be somewhat lacking in hand and arm strength, you'll enjoy using an 8- or 8½-foot rod for a 4- or 5-weight line. This type of rod weighs less than a 9-footer and will make learning easier for you. After your hand and forearm get used to casting this rod, you may want to try casting a 9-foot 6-weight rod. The 9-foot rods have a number of subtle practical advantages over shorter rods, but they can be more tiring to cast for long periods, especially for people with untempered casting muscles.

Women and kids sometimes find the typical fly-rod grip to be a bit too thick to fit comfortably in their hands. If you are trying or buying a new rod, flex it back and forth with your thumb on top of the grip to see how it feels. No matter who you are, use a rod that feels comfortable in your hand, even if you don't know what you are doing yet.

USE THE RIGHT FLY LINE

When you are first learning to cast, your fly line should be a brightly colored floating line in either a weight-forward or double taper. The weight-forward is the more versatile of the two, but the double taper is just fine if that's what you happen to

An ideal matched outfit for most flyfishers is a 9-foot 6-weight rod with a weight-forward, floating 6-weight line.

have. If you practice with a dull-colored line, it is harder to see your triumphs and errors. If you use a sinking line, its increased density can make the line unfurl abruptly and awkwardly, which will make learning harder for you. If you are using a line that is more than five years old, replace it with a new one. Fly lines degrade with age, just as windshield wiper blades do.

USE THE RIGHT LEADER

Your leader should be 7½ feet long, knotless, and taper to a 2X, 1X, or 0X tippet. (The X number is determined by subtracting the diameter of the tippet—in thousandths of an inch—from the number 11. So, a 0X tippet is .011 inches thick and a 2X is .009 inches thick; 2X tippet is therefore thinner than 0X and thicker than 4X.) Unless you already have some casting experience, don't practice casting with: (1) a leader longer than 7½ feet, (2) a leader tapering to a tippet thinner than 2X, or (3) a knotted leader (its taper is achieved by knotting together many segments of progressively thinner monofilament).

Leaders longer than 7½ feet are harder for beginners to cast, and leaders thinner than 2X may tangle. A knotted leader can tangle mercilessly for a beginner. Once you become comfortable with your fly casts, you may have plenty of fishing opportunities that call for a 10-foot knotted leader tapering to a 6X tippet. Just don't practice with one.

MAINTAIN A HAPPY LEADER

Your leader may develop simple little overhand knots—called "wind knots"—during casting (see the illustration on page 83 of Chapter 6). They are a fact of life, more so for beginners than experts, and they weaken the leader. Cut out these knots if they are in the tippet (thin) end, or undo them if they are in the butt (thick) end. When you have to cut them out of the tippet, your leader will become shorter. When it shrinks to 6 feet, use a Surgeon's Knot to add 18 inches of the appropriate tippet. For consistency, if you started with a 0X leader, add 0X tippet, and so on. For more about leaders, tippets, and knots, see the *L.L. Bean Fly-Fishing Handbook* (The Lyons Press, 1996).

USE THE RIGHT PRACTICE FLY

A leader without a practice fly is like a car without tires. To practice well, tie a piece of bright synthetic yarn onto the end of your leader using a Clinch Knot or a Duncan Loop, also called a Uni-Knot. (If you use the Clinch Knot when

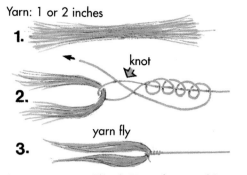

Yarn: 1 or 2 inches

1.

2. knot

3. yarn fly

You can use a Clinch Knot for attaching yarn to make your practice fly. Illustration by Dave Whitlock.

Trim your practice fly to the size of a raisin or a pea.

tying on a real fly, be sure to use the improved version.) Trim the short end of this knot as close as possible. The piece of yarn should then be trimmed to the size of a raisin or a pea. Then put fly flotant on it to make it float well. This practice fly is superior to and much cheaper than cutting the hook point off an actual fly. I wish someone had told me that when I started casting, because I neutered so many good Royal Wulffs and Elk-Hair Caddis.

MARK THE LINE

This tip has made a big difference in the learning curve of students at the L.L. Bean School in the past few years. It may seem trivial, but once you do it, you'll be glad you did. Take a permanent waterproof marker and mark a two-inch band around the line 37 feet from the tip of the line. Why 37 feet? Because holding the line at that mark will let you cast with most of the thick part of the line, called the head, outside the tip-top guide. That's the length of line that most rods are designed to cast optimally. If you add a 7½-foot leader to the line and you make a successful four-part cast (discussed in the next chapter), your fly will land

Mark the line at a point 37 feet from the tip.

45 feet away. We call that a 45-foot cast, and that's long enough to catch a lot of different kinds of fish all over the world.

ALWAYS WEAR GLASSES OR SUNGLASSES AND A HAT

Wear them when you cast and fish. Even that innocuous-looking practice fly could seriously damage your eye. I've been hit in the face many times by errant casts, mostly on windy days, and my glasses have saved my sight. The hat has saved my skin.

STRETCH THE LINE AND LEADER

Fly lines and leaders are made of sophisticated polymers, but they are not perfect. If you store them all curled up, as on a fly reel, they tend to remember the curls. It will help your casting and fishing if you get into the habit of stretching your line and leader to eliminate these curls each time you cast. The easiest way to stretch the line is to rig the rod (see Chapter 2) and have a friend pull out about 50 feet of line. You hold onto the reel while your friend holds onto the tip of the line, and the two of you simply pull for a few sec-

Stretch the line by wrapping it around a smooth object, making sure not to bend the rod.

onds. You'll feel the line stretch quite a bit as you do. Just make sure the rod is *not bent at all* during this operation, to avoid damaging it.

You can also eliminate the line curls yourself by wrapping the line around a smooth object, or by just pulling and stretching a few feet at a time between your hands.

To stretch the leader, hold the butt, or thick, end and draw the leader through your tightly clenched hand *slowly* a few times. This warms the leader as you stretch it. When you are done, you should see the leader hanging nearly straight, without pronounced coiling. Don't use a leader straightener—usually a leather or rubber pad—as this can overheat the leader and weaken it.

CLEAN THE LINE

Like bare feet on a sidewalk, most lines pick up lots of dirt. Before doing anything involving shooting, described in Chapter 6, clean your line by drawing it through a wet cloth. This will remove much of the dirt from the line and will make it float better. Next, draw it through another cloth treated with a fly-line dressing. This will make your line last longer and shoot through the guides more easily.

Eleven Habits of Highly Effective Casters

1. Practice with an 8½- or 9-foot rod designed for 5- or 6-weight line. If you lack strength in your forearm, use an 8- or 8½-foot 4- or 5-weight rod. Make sure the grip of the rod is comfortable in your hand.

2. Practice with a bright, floating line.

3. Your leader should be 7½ feet long, knotless, and tapered to a 2X, 1X, or 0X tippet.

4. Keep your leader free of knots; add tippet when it gets too short.

5. Tie synthetic yarn onto the end of your leader and trim it to the size of a pea.

6. Mark your line 37 feet from the tip.

7. Wear glasses and a hat.

8. Stretch your line and leader before you start practicing.

9. Clean the line, especially if you will be shooting line or fishing.

10. Practice wherever and whenever you can.

11. Be patient as you practice.

TO PRACTICE IS TO CELEBRATE

Practice can bring beauty to your life. Take the late Jay Gammel, a retired junior-college professor in Baytown, Texas, who had spent his leisure time hunting, fly fishing, and fly casting. On a Texas-hot day in August 1995, he was 60 years old, his spine was badly degenerated, and he had terminal lung disease. He had just been discharged from the hospital, so he could go home to die. He loved to cast so much that despite his pain and afflictions, he insisted that he cast on the day he got home. With the temperature outside at 105°F, his son helped him out to the worn place in the front yard where they had stood during their years of casting together. Jay sat down in a lawn chair and laboriously pulled the entire 90-foot fly line from the reel, followed by a few feet of backing. Unable to double haul because of his spine, he false cast and made two presentations, both times draping the practice fly over the fence at the edge of their yard. From where he sat the fence was exactly 100 feet away. "That'll do," he said. Jay went back inside, happy with his two casts. They would be his last.

Jay Gammel knew that the best place to practice is wherever you can, whenever you can.

BE PATIENT—YOU ARE NOT AN IDIOT

You'll make lots of mistakes, so don't beat up on yourself when you do. Sometimes you'll regress. There will be dips in your learning curve but, with practice, the curve will trend upward. That's all part of the learning process; every skilled flycaster has been there.

CHAPTER
2

The Four-Part Cast on a Lawn

This is the sweetest cast, the foundation of fly fishing. It is brief and almost crystalline in its simplicity. Although it is also called the overhead cast, it can be done sidearm and even underhanded.

Our goal in this chapter is to learn to count to four with a fly rod and to cast the practice fly 45 feet in the process.

At first, you should practice the four parts of this cast—pickup, backcast, forward cast, presentation—on a grassy lawn. It's easier to start on a lawn than on water. Of course, you can pantomime this cast anywhere. If you do this at work, people will think of you as someone who desperately needs a vacation.

Stand comfortably and stand up straight when you practice.

STANCE

Stand comfortably. If your feet are pointing in the general direction of your cast, that's good. Eventually, you will need to learn to cast no matter where your feet are pointing, because the stones in the river or the orientation of the boat will often dictate your stance.

Stand up straight; try not to hunch over like a great blue heron. Fishing may be life and death for the bird, but it's just fishing to you.

PANTOMIME THE CAST WITHOUT YOUR ROD

Mimic the positions you see in the photographs.

- Start with your elbow relaxed at your side, holding an imaginary rod pointing down at the water. Throughout the cast, your forearm and thumb should be aligned in a forward/backward plane, toward the fish, not off to the side.

- Mimic the pickup of the line from the water by slowly tilting your forearm toward vertical.

Start with your elbow relaxed at your side, holding an imaginary rod.

- As your imaginary rod passes through a position roughly 45 degrees above the water, accelerate it, first slowly, then briskly until your forearm snaps to a stop just short of vertical. Imagine your thumbnail pointing straight up, not back behind you. Freeze your arm there: you have just mimicked the backcast. Pause for the imaginary line to straighten in the air behind you.

Slowly tilt your forearm through the pickup, accelerating it until it snaps to a stop, just short of vertical. Your thumbnail should be pointing straight up.

• Begin the forward cast with your forearm simply reversing its course, starting slowly but accelerating to an abrupt stop at a position *above* the horizon.

Starting slowly, accelerate the forward cast to an abrupt stop, with your forearm stopping at the 45-degree position.

- Once your arm has totally stopped, gently lower your forearm to the ground as your imaginary line unrolls in the air and falls. We call this the presentation, or delivery.
- Practice this at least ten times.

Gently lower your forearm to the ground as your imaginary line unrolls in the air and falls.

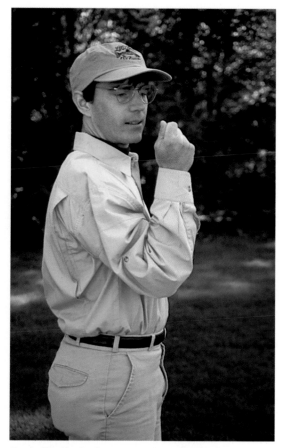

You may prefer to lift your elbow slightly, no more than 3 or 4 inches, during the backcast.

Periodically look at your thumbnail. It should be pointing straight up at the backcast stop.

Many casters prefer to lift their elbow slightly (no more than 3 or 4 inches) during the backcast, and to pull the elbow back down to their side during the forward cast. The longer the cast, the more you will need to raise your elbow. While it is not always necessary to do this during a 45-foot cast, you will need to do so to make longer casts and crisp roll casts. In search of elegance and a quiet body when casting, I raise my elbow no more than I have to. Whether you choose this style during the short casts is something for you to decide. Try it both ways; choose the one that feels best.

Casting Is Counterintuitive

A good fly cast is counterintuitive. Our natural tendency is to wave the rod through a wide arc when casting. Perhaps the most challenging part of the cast is resisting the temptation to do this. In the beginning you'll have to "stop short," particularly during the backcast. In most casting, doing less with the rod usually means getting more from the cast.

At the forward cast stop, you should see your thumbnail pointing up at about a 45-degree angle in the sky, not straight at the horizon. You should also see your forearm pointing above the horizon.

Don't do this. Straightening your arm during the forward cast is awkward, tiring, and will undermine your ability to make long casts someday.

As you'll see in the photographs in this book, casting is not robotic. Even a highly skilled caster displays some variation in style, even over the course of a few minutes. Casts are like snowflakes—no two are truly identical.

Do ten more casts. Periodically, when you stop after your backcast, turn your head and *look at your thumbnail*. It should be pointing straight up. Look at your elbow. It should be either relaxed at your side or elevated slightly in front of you. When you stop after your forward cast, look at your thumbnail: you should see it pointing up at about a 45-degree angle in the sky, not straight at the horizon. You should also see your forearm and upper arm form about a 45- to a 90-degree angle. Do *not* straighten your arm during the forward cast. Doing so is laborious, tiring, and will undermine your ability to make long casts someday.

What Is Muscle Memory?

Muscle memory is the ability of your muscles to repeat a motion without your thinking about it, because of many repetitions in the past. It's what allows you to walk while chewing gum, to ride a bicycle or serve a tennis ball. The pantomime will help you to do the casting motion correctly with enough repetition that your muscles will remember what to do, even when you are not paying attention. This will let you relax and even daydream as you fish, enriching your fishing experience and ensuring that, during your reverie, some of the big ones will get away.

By doing this pantomime, you are educating your muscles and giving them a memory of what the cast requires.

Now you're ready to pick up the rod.

HOLD THE ROD

Your thumb should be on the grip with your index finger opposite your thumb. Don't forget this or you'll have trouble stopping the rod on the backcast. Now, squeeze the grip hard, very hard. Good. *Never do that again.* Your grip should be relaxed, something that you can do for hours on end with no strain.

Keep your thumb on the grip. This will let you accelerate the rod on the forward cast and stop the rod on the backcast.

Holding the rod this way will result in bad fly casts.

Cast with the rod tilted slightly off vertical.

TILT THE ROD

Tilt it slightly off to the side while pointing it up. This will usually keep the line from hitting the rod and will prevent the unsettling sight of the fly coming at your head at 60 mph. If the line hits the rod often, or if you flinch each time the fly hurtles past you, tilt the rod even further to the side.

FLEX THE ROD

Flex it back and forth with no line. Move the handle

very little while making the rest of the rod flex a lot. (It may help you to put your left hand on the end of the rod as an anchor point.) You can see how making a relatively compact motion with your hand and forearm can translate into a big motion in the rod.

Notice that it's easier to do this when your elbow is close to your side and your hand is slightly in front of you. Now hold the rod up in the Statue of Liberty position and try the same thing. That's harder, isn't it? *Casting is easier when you keep your rod hand and your elbow very close to your body.*

PANTOMIME WITH AN UNRIGGED ROD

Repeat the casting pantomime sequence you did earlier, but this time do it while holding the rod. Do this at least ten times, carefully, deliberately:

1. Pick up slowly.
2. Transition smoothly into the backcast; pause.
3. Make the forward cast.
4. Lower the rod to the ground for the presentation.

Every cast begins and ends with the rod tip nearly touching the water.

Do the four-part cast ten more times while going through the same checklist you did earlier:

- Begin and end every cast with the rod tip nearly touching the water.
- Check your thumb position after the backcast stop.
- Make sure your rod freezes as you wait for the would-be line to unroll behind you.
- Be sure your elbow is either relaxed or slightly in front of you during this time.
- At the end of the forward cast, your rod should completely stop and it should be pointing up in the sky; your forearm should be pointing above the horizon.
- Lower your rod gently after this stop as the imaginary line falls to the ground.

At the backcast stop, be sure your elbow is either relaxed or slightly in front of you.

At the end of the forward cast, your rod and forearm should be pointing up.

For the presentation, slowly lower your rod tip after the forward cast comes to a complete stop.

If you've noticed how short a distance the rod is moving, you're doing just fine. Remember, the less you move the rod, the more you'll get from the cast. Also, notice that your hand is lower after the forward-cast stop than after the backcast stop. This is as it should be.

Now, do the cast ten more times, making sure to start each cast slowly, but accelerating the rod to an abrupt stop at the end of the cast. This applies to both the forward and backcasts. *This acceleration to a stop is the single most important thing you do with a fly rod. Without it, the cast cannot happen.* It means that every backcast you make starts with a *whimper* and ends with a relative *bang,* and that every forward cast you make starts with a *whimper* and ends with a relative *bang.*

CASTING A LINE FOR THE FIRST TIME

- Pull line off the reel until you expose your 37-foot mark.
- String the line through the guides by doubling over the tip of the line. We call this a rigged rod. Now lay your rod down so it points in your casting direction.
- Pull all that line straight out through the guides and lay it down so it is still straight. Stretch the line and leader as described earlier.

What Does Acceleration-to-a-Stop Feel Like?

With graphite fly rods, the acceleration to a stop often feels more like a two-speed stroke—slow, then flick—than a gradual acceleration. Many casters describe a "twitch," "pop," or "snap" at the very end of the backcast and forward cast. Depending on the length of line you are casting and the weight of the rod, this will feel like anything from a twitch—a quick contraction of your hand and forearm muscles—to a thrust of energy. I think of the end of the acceleration as a **pop/stop: pop**, as the last tiny burst of acceleration; and **stop**, because the stroke must end. To do the right thing, try these analogies:

1. Still without a line on your rod, try to cast the *tip* section off the *butt* of the rod. Try to do it during the backcast and then during the forward cast. (The butt is the thick end of the rod.)
2. Put an inch of water in a cup. Hold it as though you are about to make a forward cast. Now, mimic the cast, trying to cast the water as far forward as possible. If most of the water went out in front of you, you did the right thing. If most of the water went up in the air, you accelerated too abruptly. (Don't try this indoors.)

If you ease forward and pop/stop, most of the water will fly out in front of you.

If you pop too soon, most of the water will go up in the air.

- Pick up the rod, making sure to keep the tip pointed *down,* because most fly casts begin and end with the rod tip pointing at the water.

- Pin your mark against the grip with your index finger, your middle finger, or both, leaving a 2-foot loop of line hanging down between your rod hand and the reel. We'll use this loop later when we begin to strip line. Your other hand, called the line hand, can just hang at your side.

String the line through the guides by doubling over the tip of the line.

Pin the marked line against the grip.

If there is a breeze, position yourself so the wind is blowing perpendicular to the rod and the rod is on your downwind side.

IS THERE A BREEZE?

If so, position yourself accordingly. Just turn yourself so that your rod hand is on your *downwind* side, with the rod pointing perpendicular to the wind. This will prevent the wind from blowing the line into you or your rod during the backcast or forward cast.

PICKUP

Until you get to Chapter 6, begin *every* cast with the line fully extended, straight out in front of you, with the rod tip practically touching the ground. Gently lift the rod tip by tilting your forearm upward, keeping your elbow

Begin every cast with the line fully extended and the rod tip practically touching the ground.

As the rod passes through the 45-degree position, begin your backcast. There should be no hesitation or "hitch" between your pickup and backcast.

close to your side. Increase the speed at which the rod tip sweeps up. When the rod passes through the 45-degree position, begin your backcast. The pickup and backcast are different phases of the cast, but they should feel to you as one smooth motion. There is no hesitation or "hitch" between the pickup and backcast.

BACKCAST

The backcast flows smoothly from the pickup, with the rod accelerating from a whimper at 45 degrees to an abrupt pop/stop just beyond vertical.

PAUSE

Let the line straighten behind you. Try to anticipate when the line will completely straighten behind you, and start your forward cast just before. You should not feel a tug when the line straightens behind you. If you do, your fly is either too heavy for casting practice or you neglected to tie on a leader.

Accelerate the rod to a pop/stop.

Pause to allow the line time to fully straighten behind you.

FORWARD CAST

This is the exact opposite of the backcast. Start slowly, accelerating to an abrupt stop, with the rod stopping about 45 degrees above the horizon. Remember, *the forward cast has no more and no less energy than the backcast.* It should move at the same speed and acceleration as the backcast.

Accelerate the rod forward to a pop/stop.

Stop the rod completely at the end of the forward cast. The loop of line flying off the tip is described in Chapter 5.

PRESENTATION

After the rod has completely stopped at the end of the forward cast, let gravity lower the rod tip along with the line as it falls to the water. This is a gentle motion. You are simply allowing the tip to drop with the line. At the end of the presentation, the rod tip should nearly touch the ground. If your line is nearly straight on the ground in front of you, that's great! Keep doing it.

As the line unfurls and is pulled to the ground by gravity, slowly lower your rod tip to the ground. The tip should fall as the line falls.

Among other things, you may notice that your hand is lower after stopping the forward cast than after stopping the backcast. Don't worry; this is the way it should be.

During the forward cast, your hand should travel down.

At this stage, try not to practice more than 20 minutes at a time. Without a casting instructor present, your concentration may flag and you may develop some bad habits.

Why Is the Acceleration-to-a-Stop So Important?

When your backcast or forward cast is viewed from the side, the tip of your rod should appear to move in a straight line. By starting slowly and accelerating to a pop/stop, your rod tip will move this way. If you don't accelerate at the end, or if you accelerate only in the beginning and slow down to a stop, the rod tip will move in a lazy, convex path and the cast will be ineffective.

The progressive acceleration to an abrupt stop over a short arc is what makes the rod tip travel in a straight line and makes the cast successful.

This caster never accelerated the rod, so the tip didn't bend. The line followed the tip through the convex arc, resulting in a poor cast.

How Does Your Arm Make the Acceleration-to-a-Stop Happen?

During the cast, two things happen sequentially. As your forearm accelerates toward the stop, your rod bends (or "loads") against the weight of fly line in the air. What causes the rod to pop to a stop is that your wrist kicks in just a *little* bit at the end of your forearm's journey while the forearm twitches. Even though your wrist moves during the pop, it stops the rod just beyond vertical (backcast) and at 45 degrees above the horizon (forward cast). During a typical 45-foot backcast or forward cast, this sequence takes less than one second and should feel as one continuous motion. If you feel as if you are drowning in details right now, just move the rod from the start to the stop, starting slowly and speeding up to a pop/stop.

This is a wristy cast. The angler's rod is at the backcast stop, but his forearm is at the forward cast stop. This casting style will severely limit your fly-fishing horizons.

PLAYING AROUND

- **Close Your Eyes.** For some reason, many people cast better with their eyes closed. There are no visual distractions. Give it a try!

- **The Line Slam.** Make a backcast and forward cast in which you try to make the line slam into the rod. The line probably won't hit the rod, but you will make a successful cast. This can be helpful if you've had trouble conceptualizing the pop/stop.

• **The Belly Cast.** This is not some cruel joke to get your neighbors to laugh at you. First, lie down with the line pinned against the grip and fully extended in front of you. While leaning on your elbows, make some four-part casts. As always, start with the rod tip low to the ground, and make several four-part casts: *pickup, backcast, forward cast, presentation.* Keeping your elbows on the ground, remember to bring your forearm almost to vertical while accelerating to a pop/stop; point your thumb straight up at the backcast stop; pause; accelerate to a pop/stop during

Keeping your elbow on the ground at all times, make a belly cast. The backcast is the same as during a conventional four-part cast . . .

. . . as are the stop positions.

the forward cast; allow your forearm and rod to return to horizontal during the presentation. Yes, it sounds weird, but it's a really fun way to learn to cast with a minimum of wasted motion. It also proves that casting is the same whether you are wading in a river or fishing from a canoe or float tube.

TROUBLESHOOTING

Videotaping yourself can be very helpful if you are having some troubles. The tape can expose most of the following errors to your view:

Five Common Problems

1. **Why isn't the line straightening out in front?**
   - You may have forgotten to start every cast with the line fully extended on the ground, straight in front of you.
   - You may be popping the rod too far back during your backcast. This will cast the line down toward the ground behind you and, consequently, up on the next forward cast. To fix this, attempt to stop your rod nearly vertically during the backcast, still with the pop/stop. Your next forward cast will then have a much better chance of straightening out.
   - You may be pausing too long before you start your forward cast, which allows your backcast to fall near the ground. This sends your forward cast up high, and makes it fall in a heap.
   - You may not be accelerating to a pop/stop at all, causing the rod tip to move too slowly at the end of the cast.
   - You may be accelerating to a pop/stop with too much force, causing the line to bounce back after it has fully extended in the air.
   - You may be starting your forward cast with too much speed, which sends the line up high in the air, and then into another heap. Remember, start slowly.

2. **You hear a noise like a snapping bullwhip during your forward cast.** This happens when you start your forward cast too soon, before the backcast has had time to fully straighten. To correct this, pause a little longer between the backcast and forward cast.

3. **The line keeps hitting you or the rod.** This usually happens because there is a crosswind blowing the line into you or the rod on either the

forward cast or backcast. To fix it, rotate your body so the rod is on the downwind side of your body. Be sure to cast with the rod tilted slightly off to the side, away from vertical.

4. **You hear a whooshing noise during the backcast.** You are probably accelerating the backcast quickly rather than slowly. Start *slowly.* Remember that the rod goes fast only at the end of the cast, not at the beginning. You may also be moving the rod through a very long arc. Keep the casting arc short by stopping your backcast just *barely* beyond vertical.

5. **Your casting hand is getting tired.** Take a break. Massage your casting hand with your line hand. This may be a good time to start living dangerously—try casting with your *other* hand. For more about this, see **Playing Around** in Chapter 4.

CHAPTER 3

The Roll Cast

All the casts in this book feel good, but a roll cast has a special feeling. When I first started teaching casting, this was one cast that still didn't feel right: It took a lot of energy but yielded little in return. With practice and some guidance from another instructor, I soon had my roll casts leaping off the rod tip and unfurling above the water.

The roll cast is really a modified forward cast without a backcast: It's a four-part cast without the first two parts. You'll use it when you can't make a backcast because of obstructions behind you, or when your line is in a heap on water in front of you. It can also be used to pick up line from the water in preparation for a backcast (described in Chapter 7). Many beginners treat this as a baby cast, but it isn't. You will use the roll cast countless times during a typical fishing day.

GETTING LINE ON THE WATER

Roll casts must have resistance to work properly. Unless you use a clipboard to hold the fly, you can't practice this successfully on the lawn. To get started on the water, pull line off the reel until you get a couple of feet past your 37-foot mark. With the leader, fly, and a few feet

Allagash River, Northern Maine

You are picking your way along the rocky, wooded shore of Maine's remote Allagash River. There is no room behind you for a backcast. Small brook trout are rising splashily to caddisflies emerging on the surface. You make short roll casts to them with your size 14 Elk Hair Caddis on 4X tippet. This is only a vague imitation of what the fish are eating, but they are unsophisticated and rise to your fly with abandon. Brook trout have been in this remote river since the last Ice Age, but they look as if they just came from an Expressionist painting. They have brilliant orange bellies and creamy white edges on their delicate fins. Their vermiculated flanks look like an artist's brooding abstraction. You catch many of them, and you have only read as far as the Roll Cast chapter in this book.

of line on the water, point your rod down at the water and make quick, aggressive sweeps of the rod, back and forth with the rod tip barely above the water. This motion is the same one we used earlier (in Chapter 2), when we flexed the rod back and forth with no line—we moved the grip very little, while making the rest of the rod flex a lot. With a little line on the water, this will cause all the rest of the line to swish out through the guides onto the surface. Once you get the leader and tip of the line on the water, the whole operation should take no more than five seconds. Now, pin the mark against the grip, leaving a 2-foot loop to hang between your rod hand and the reel.

For roll casting on a lawn, use a clipboard to hold your practice fly. Otherwise, your roll casts will fall in a heap.

To get the line onto the water, keep the rod tip barely above the water and make long, aggressive snaps of the rod, back and forth.

To set up for a roll cast, slowly drag the line and fly into position.

SETUP

This is done *very slowly*. You are not making a backcast; you are gently moving the rod into position behind you to make the roll cast. To do it, draw the rod to the backcast position, but in ultra-slow motion. Your rod should move in a single plane, tilted slightly off to the side, just as during the standard pickup and backcast. The leader and fly never leave the water; they just get dragged slowly along the surface as you move the rod into the setup position. If you notice that your setup is causing the leader and fly to lift off the water, slow down your setup. The roll cast is easier if you raise your elbow somewhat, so your upper arm generally points toward the fish.

Move the rod to the backcast stop position. Raise your upper arm and point it out toward the fish. The rod and line form a tilted "D."

PAUSE

Wait with the rod motionless at the backcast-stop position for about three seconds until the line has stopped moving behind you. Before you come forward, you should see your rod and line form a "D." (Look for a reverse "D" if you are left-handed.)

ROLL CAST

- As with the four-part cast, the rod should travel in the same plane throughout the cast: it should not curve or sweep to the side.

- Start forward very slowly by pulling *down* with your elbow and hand. As you do this, your forearm and rod should tilt forward. As your rod moves through the vertical position, accelerate hard to a pop/stop, somewhere near 45 degrees above the horizon.

- Compared to the forward casts you did earlier, the roll cast starts more gently but ends even more emphatically, with a harder pop/stop. This is because, unlike the forward cast, you have to make the line overcome the drag of the water before it gets airborne.

Start by slowly pulling down with your elbow and hand to tilt the rod forward.

As your rod moves through the vertical position, accelerate hard.

The roll cast pop/stop is even more emphatic than it is in the forward snap of a four-part cast. In particular, the pop feels like an electric pulse, a spasm of the forearm. Your hand may only travel 3 or 4 inches during this pop, or burst.

Except on very long roll casts, stop the butt somewhere above the horizon.

- When you finish, you should once again see your rod and your forearm pointing somewhere above the horizon, with your elbow very close to your body. As in the four-part cast, a loop of line will fly off your rod tip immediately after the abrupt stop.

The end of the roll cast looks like the forward portion of a four-part cast because it is a forward cast, without a backcast.

PRESENTATION

You've been here before. As the roll cast unfurls and the line falls, lower your rod tip along with it.

PLAYING AROUND

- **Off-Shoulder Roll Cast.** Remember in Chapter 2, when you positioned yourself so that the rod was on the downwind side of any crosswind? Well, now that you are on the water, you don't have that luxury: the water is where it is. What you *can* change is where the tip of the rod travels. You can practice this even when there is no wind.

  Imagine that you have a crosswind blowing from right to left. Tilt the rod over your head so the tiptop and the line travel on your downwind side. How? Instead of tilting your forearm away from you while keeping your elbow in close to your side, do the opposite. Push your elbow out from your side and bring your hand in close to your ear. This will tilt your rod over the top of your head. This keeps your hand on your right side, where it is strongest, and puts the rod tip over your left shoulder. This

For the off-shoulder roll cast, push your elbow out from your side and bring your hand in close to your ear. This will tilt your rod over the top of your head.

position ensures that the wind will blow the line away from you instead of into you. Otherwise, the roll cast is done exactly as you did it before.

- **Two-Handed Roll Casting.** If you're struggling with the roll cast or your arm is just tired, you can use two hands to roll cast. Simply put your left hand on the end of the rod and do the roll cast. You'll find it much easier to pop/stop the rod, and you may be dazzled by the results. I use two hands whenever I need to make a long roll cast. Also, this is a great

The two-handed roll cast turbocharges your roll cast. It's great when you're using a heavy outfit, when it's windy, or when you need a long cast.

technique for children, whose arms often lack the strength to accelerate and stop a rod properly during both the roll cast and the four-part cast.

TROUBLESHOOTING

Four Common Problems

1. **The line piles in front of you.** You either started the forward cast with too much acceleration before ending too slowly, or your pop came too late in the cast, driving the unfurling line down into the water instead of over the water.

2. **Your line unrolls only partially.** This probably means you need more energy throughout your forward stroke. Start the roll cast more forcefully, but remember that you need the abrupt pop at the end of the stroke.

3. **It's windy.** End your roll cast stroke farther down, close to the horizon. This will help drive the cast under the wind, giving it less "sail area." When you do this, you'll need to make the first part of the stroke move a little faster than normal.

4. **The line is hitting you or tangling on itself.** Even if there is no wind, this can happen when the caster is positioned between the line and the path of the rod. For example, if you are trying to roll cast the line straight out from your position while the line is to your left, a conventional roll cast will cause the line to hit you. Try it: You'll be kissed by a wet practice fly. To compensate, use the off-shoulder roll cast. Tilt your elbow out and your hand in, putting the rod tip over your left shoulder. Make the cast.

Roll Casting for Corporate CEOs and Other Overachievers

The Spey rod, named for a famous salmon river in Scotland, is a two-handed rod that enables skilled casters to roll cast specialized lines beyond 80 feet! Done properly, it is beautiful to watch and enables its practitioners to reach distant salmon when fishing in front of a steep or wooded streambank. The physics are the same as with a typical roll cast, but the rod feels ungainly at first. The proper technique takes considerable patience to master. Like single-malt Scotch, Spey casting is an acquired taste.

Casting as Daydreaming

If all this casting detail seems mentally taxing, you're not alone. Except for the gifted few (I was not a member of this group), this is a lot to remember at first. But, just like learning to drive a car, you'll notice that as you practice, you'll think less and less while you cast better and better. Eventually you'll find yourself daydreaming as you cast and fish, your mind drifting off into woods or up into sky. These times are often interrupted by the fish.

If you try to roll cast the line straight out from your position while the line is to your left . . .

. . . the result will be ugly. Use the off-shoulder roll cast instead.

CHAPTER 4

The Four-Part Cast on the Water

The four-part cast is the bread-and-butter cast, the one that trout guides pray their clients can make. From what we know, the cast has not changed much since Dame Juliana Berners wrote the first fly-fishing book in 1496. It is, of course, easier to do this cast now, with modern rods and lines, than it was in her time. But learning it still requires patience and practice.

In this chapter, we build on what you have done in the first three. The only new twist is that you have to develop a smooth pickup from the water, one that transitions into a nearly vertical backcast.

STANCE

Imagine that you are at a party, talking to a 5-foot-tall fish. That's how you should stand.

PICKUP

Begin every pickup with the line fully extended, straight out in front of you, with the rod tip

Yellowstone Lake, Northwestern Wyoming

You are standing on the shore of Yellowstone Lake in Yellowstone National Park. The surface of the huge lake is a boundless mirror, reflecting the volcanic mountains to the east. Large cutthroat trout cruise the shoreline searching and rising for *Callibaetis*, a speckled-wing mayfly. You are fishing with a size 16 Sparkle Dun and tiny 6X tippet. You make simple four-part casts of just 30 feet, then you watch your fly sit motionless on the mirror for a long time. You see rises here and there as you wait, watching your fly. You gaze up at the mountains in the distance. There is a noise, a disturbance where your fly was sitting, so you raise the rod tip to set the hook, but the fish is already gone. They will be rising for hours. It is a beautiful day.

Begin every pickup with the line fully extended and the rod tip nearly touching the water.

pointing down at the water. The pickup is much more important when you are lifting the line from the water than when you are lifting it from land. Water has surface tension that holds onto the line as you try to pick it up. The pickup requires you to *ease* the line *gently* from the water and transition smoothly into the backcast. Again, this will look and feel as one smooth motion. The motion is just as it was on land except that your rod will now bend more against the drag of the water on the line. The pickup ends and the backcast begins the moment you see the end of the fly line lift off the water, usually when your rod is pointing about 45 degrees above the water.

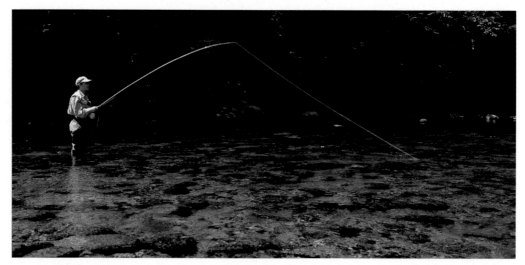

From a gentle pickup, transition smoothly into the backcast.

The backcast, forward cast, and presentation are exactly the same over the water as they are over the lawn. Do as many repetitions of this four-part cast as you can.

The Sound of Silence

Most good fly casts are virtually silent. If you hear a tearing sound during the pickup, a whooshing sound during the backcast, or a whistling sound during your forward cast, see "Troubleshooting" at the end of this chapter.

Accelerate the rod . . .

. . . to an abrupt stop. Pause to allow the line to unfurl behind you.

Accelerate the forward cast to a pop/stop about 45 degrees above the horizon.

Gently lower the rod tip, along with the falling line, to the water.

Watch the practice fly land on the water with the line fully extended. If it's not fully extended, see "Troubleshooting."

INVERT THE REEL

This is a test to make sure you are using your forearm in the cast. Simply invert the reel and make some casts with it butting up against the underside of your forearm. (Make sure the reel touches your forearm at the backcast stop.) Actually, you could have snuck this far into the learning process by casting

What Do the Start and Stop Feel Like?

During the **backcast,** you'll pull against your index finger and push against the butt of your hand. When you make the **backcast stop,** your thumb enforces the stop. The backcast stop should look as if your rod has hit an invisible wall. Your thumb and two smallest fingers make that wall.

During the **forward cast,** you'll push with your thumb and pull with your two smallest fingers. At the **forward-cast stop,** stop the rod with your index finger and the butt of your hand. A good way to feel this is to pantomime with the unrigged rod again.

Your thumb and two smallest fingers enforce the backcast stop. They keep the rod from tipping back further. The backcast stop should look as if your rod has hit an invisible wall.

Your index finger and the butt of your hand enforce the forward-cast stop.

The Power Snap or Pop/Stop

Fly rods have become stiffer over the years as a result of changing preferences and the advent of space-age materials, so the transition from slow to pop/stop has become more abrupt. When my students put their hands on mine to get the feel of how I cast, some of them say that the pop/stop feels like a jerk. If we were using the old bamboo rods, they would feel a more gradual final acceleration. They might then say, "It feels as if you're speeding up and then stopping." If you're curious about how this would feel, cast an 8-weight fly line on a 5-weight rod. The relatively heavy 8-weight line will cause the light 5-weight rod to bend more and react more slowly to your casting motion than a 5-weight line would.

What About Watching Your Backcast?

Advanced casters will sometimes watch their backcast to improve their casts. They are able to turn their heads to watch without being distracted. They know what they are looking for in their backcast and can use what they learn from seeing only one backcast to improve the next one. On the other hand, novice casters already have a lot on their minds and are unlikely to benefit from this yet. In novices, the practice can lead to the unconscious habit of repeatedly looking at some nebulous area up in the sky for the purpose of "watching the backcast." This complicates the cast. Once you have mastered the double haul and can comfortably cast beyond 60 feet, you can learn a lot from watching your backcast. Until then, avoid it.

---

mostly with your wrist. This would be fine if you never planned to fish anything heavier than a 5-weight and never planned to cast more than 45 feet. In short, it limits your fishing horizons. Casting with the inverted reel forces you to get in the habit of bending at the elbow and casting with your forearm.

PLAYING AROUND

- **Cast with your other hand.** This is not only a good way to rest your casting arm, it is a great way to learn.

  Strange but true, most fly casters are better casters with their off hands than with their dominant hands. That is, they make more elegant casts than they do with their dominant hands. Why?

To ensure that you are casting primarily with your forearm, try casting with the reel butting up against the underside of your forearm. Make sure the reel stays there at the backcast stop.

Your off hand is a clean slate. It has no bad casting habits, no bad golf-swing habit, no tennis memory. It is a true novice. It usually learns to cast faster and better than your dominant arm. Once it does so, it trains the other side to do better. How? Only your cognitive psychologist knows for sure. But it is a joy to watch our Fly-Fishing School students cast beautifully with their off hand after protesting, "I can't do *anything* with my left hand." This may sound like New-Age logic, but you *have* to try it!

- **Close your eyes.** This is another New-Age drill that works. Like casting with the other hand, it leads many novice casters to breakthroughs. It will let you fish with confidence at night, when big striped bass and brown trout are feeding heavily. Again, you just *have* to try this!

- **Use two hands.** Pin the line against the grip, put your left hand on the butt end, and cast with two hands as you did with two-handed roll casting. Notice how easy it is to accelerate the rod to a pop/stop.

TROUBLESHOOTING

Six Common Problems

1. **Your fly lands after the line has landed.** So what? The fish don't notice and, more important, they don't care. The notion that the fly must land before the line does is folklore, probably invented by someone who wanted to exclude newcomers from the sport. (That said, it is *fun* to make the fly land before the line, and there is one very specialized fishing situation that calls for it. To learn how, see "Playing Around" in Chapter 5.)

Differences in Casting Style

The more you cast and fish, the more you'll see fly fishers who don't cast the way you do. In fact, judging by what you've learned in these pages, you'll see many whose casting looks all wrong. They use too little forearm or they move their elbows or shoulders a lot. They may bring the rod back too far during the backcast or drive the rod down to the horizon during the forward cast. Many of them struggle to get the fly to the fish. But, you'll notice that some of these people who cast "incorrectly" nonetheless get the line to lay out beautifully on the water. They have learned how to compensate for inefficiencies in their casting style. Or maybe they never liked the feel of the most efficient cast. Maybe they just like to move their bodies more than you or I do while they fish. The difference between what they do and what you do is just that you are more efficient than they are: You cast with less energy and less effort than they do. They have become comfortable with their casting style, even though their casts burn more calories than yours do. This doesn't mean that they are less effective than you, however. I've seen countless ugly casts yield beautiful fish. Most important, these anglers love fishing just as much as you do.

This is not the intended result.

2. **Your line isn't extending fully.** This one is serious. See "Troubleshooting" in Chapter 2.
3. **Your leader looks as if it's been attacked by a cat.** It's kinky and riddled with wind knots and your casts aren't straightening out. It's time to attach a new leader with either a Nail Knot or Loop-to-Loop Connection. (The Nail Knot is better for casting and fishing, but the Loop-to-Loop is easier to do.)

An abrupt pickup has ripped line and water from the surface, making a hissing, tearing sound. If you hear this sound, ease the line up from the water and transition smoothly into the backcast. Wait until you see the tip of the fly line lift off the water before you start the backcast.

4. **You hear a tearing or ripping sound during the pickup.** It is common for beginners to try to yank or rip the line up off the water. A good test of whether your pickup is too fast is when you hear the line come off the water. An abrupt pickup makes a tearing or hissing sound as the line chaotically rips water from the surface. If you hear this sound, slow down your pickup. *Ease* the line up from the water, and transition smoothly into the backcast just as you see the tip of the fly line lift off the water. Practice overcompensation; pick up the line *too* slowly. Do it again and again. Get used to the sound of silence as you pick up the line.

5. **You hear a whooshing noise during the backcast.** You are probably beginning the backcast too abruptly. Start *slowly*. Remember that the rod goes fast only at the end of the cast, not at the beginning. You may also be moving the rod through a very long arc. Keep the casting arc short by stopping your backcast at a point barely past vertical.

6. **You hear a whistling or hissing noise during the forward cast.** This should only happen when you are casting ultra-long distances. If you hear a hiss during a 45-foot cast, you need to slow down your forward cast. Remember that it should travel at the same speed as your backcast. Practice overcompensation: Make a forward cast that has all the correct hand, arm, and rod positions *and* that has the pop/stop, but that moves *too* slowly. Make your forward cast so slow that the line coming off the rod tip can't fully unfurl in front. Practice this until your typical forward cast quiets down.

CHAPTER
5

False Casting

This is the beauty cast, the signature cast of our sport, appearing to non-anglers as a waving back and forth of the rod and line. In fact, "false cast" is a misnomer. This is a true cast, but it is made in the air and not presented to the fish. It is simply a backcast and forward cast repeated without interruption by a presentation.

We use a false cast to:

- blow-dry a waterlogged fly.
- perform an in-air change of our fishing direction.
- lengthen the cast in the air (when combined with the shooting technique you'll learn in the next chapter).

A false cast can be performed anywhere: it is as lovely on a grassy lawn as on a rumbling river.

In this chapter you'll learn how to false cast, and how to use that as a stepping stone to longer casts. You'll also learn about the loop of line that you flick off the rod tip

San Juan River, New Mexico

You are fishing the San Juan River in northern New Mexico. It holds 20,000 big, fat rainbow trout per mile, and it seems that most of them are rising right in front of you. Predictably, there is a steady emergence of tiny, size 20 *Baetis* mayflies on this snowy noon in January; your Sparkle Dun is a good imitation. Even though there is ice in your guides, your 8½-foot 3-weight rod, 11-foot leader and 6X tippet allow you to rhythmically place your fly upstream of the rainbow snouts sipping insects in the surface film.

You've just caught your second fish; the fly has become waterlogged during the struggle. Your hands are too cold to tie on a new fly, one that's dry and buoyant. Instead, you false cast a few times to shake some water off the fly, then place it in front of the feeding rainbows. The fly is barely floating. A fish takes it but you try to set the hook too quickly and miss. The fly starts to sink. A few more aggressive false casts dry out the fly just enough so you can get one more good drift and a shot at just one more fish. That's all you ask, just one more.

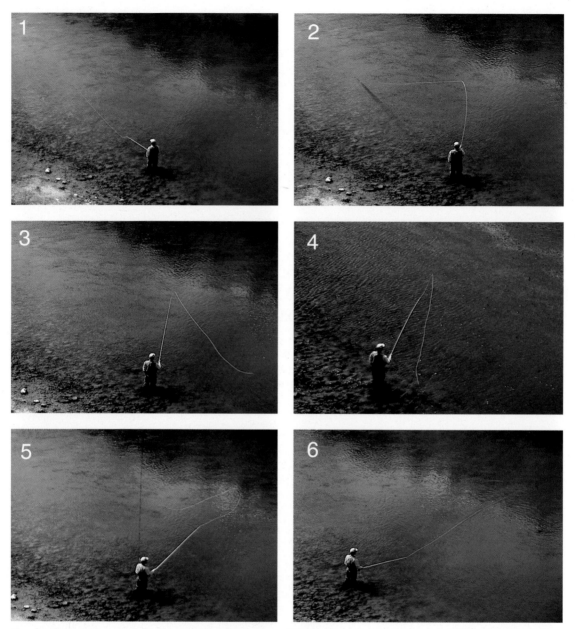

By slowly rotating your body as you make a series of three false casts, you can move the fly from the position in figure 1 to the position in figure 6, while preventing the fly and line from slapping the water.

each time you stop the rod. (In false casting, you make a lot of these loops quickly.) Finally, you'll enjoy the hypnotic rhythm of false casting: time seems to be suspended while you are practicing it.

HOW TO FALSE CAST

- Pin the line against the grip at the 37-foot mark.

- Keeping the rod tilted slightly off to the side, make your usual pickup; ease the line off the water and accelerate to your normal pop/stop backcast.

- After the stop, freeze your rod. (Do not let it creep forward during the pause.) Then make your forward cast—it is an exact reversal of the backcast.

- After the rod stops on the forward cast, freeze your rod in that position. Keep it motionless until you see the leader almost fully unfurl in front of you.

- Just before the leader is about to straighten, make your backcast, accelerating to your habitual pop/stop, making sure to stop your backcast *exactly* where you stop all your other backcasts.

- Continue this for a total of three false casts—three backcasts and three forward casts.

- As the third successive forward cast is unfurling, make the presentation, lowering the rod tip to the water exactly as you have done many times before. Your fly should not have touched the water during the false casts.

Your last forward cast should stop exactly where your first forward cast did, just where it does during the four-part cast. Remember, all backcasts and forward casts during false casting have the same amount of energy and acceleration as they do in your four-part casts. *All* your backcasts and forward casts should stop in the same place as they do in your four-part casts.

Some people freak out and seem to lose body control during false casting. When the line is in the air, they feel like Atlas holding up the world. If this sounds like you:

- Relax and take a deep breath before you start.

- As usual, keep the rod tilted slightly away from you.

- Concentrate on just making the next cast; don't worry about the line. Don't think about keeping the line up in the air. You just have to keep making the next cast.

- Freeze the rod after each stop to let the line unfurl, just as you did in the four-part cast.

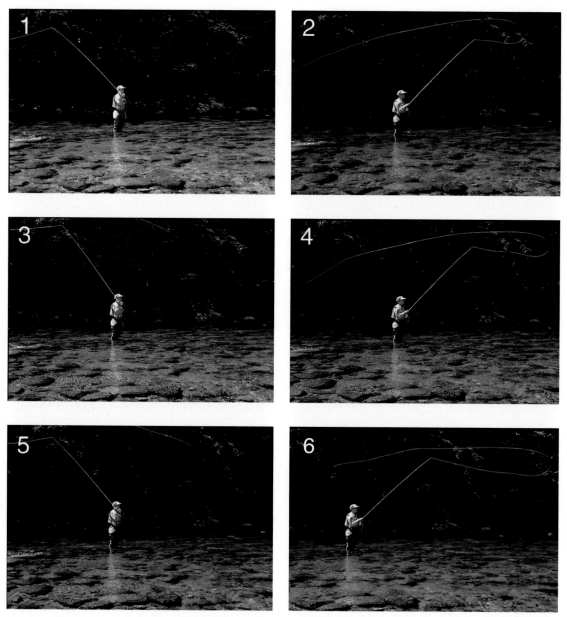

Here is a series of three false casts. Until you begin to shoot line in the next chapter, every backcast, as shown in figures 1, 3, and 5, should stop in the same place, as should every forward cast, as in figures 2, 4, and 6.

- Just before the line fully straightens, make the next cast.
- If the cast blows up, that's okay. You're fly casting and entropy sometimes wins.
- You may find it easier to pantomime the false cast with only your hand before you try it again with a rigged rod.

Remember that learning means making lots of mistakes, so be patient when false casting. Just keep at it, taking deep breaths or laughing when you get fouled up. Walk yourself through the instructions again if things aren't going well. Now may

> ### A Minimalist Goes Fly Casting
>
> Minimalism is elegance. It is casting with a quiet body, one that wastes no motion on the cast. So, teach your muscles to do the least possible to make each false cast. If you can teach them do very little now, they will have room to do much more when you learn to cast longer distances.

be a good time to set up the video camera to help analyze what you're doing, as discussed in the next chapter.

WHY ONLY THREE FALSE CASTS?

You should keep things simple, especially in the beginning. To false cast incessantly is to invite entropy, the principle of physics which tells us that things ultimately fall apart. It's like playing with fire: It can be alluring and mesmerizing but eventually you *will* get burned. The line may hit the rod, tangle on itself, or just self-destruct. When you are fishing with a real hook on the leader, there is an even greater chance of this happening. So, in the beginning, limit yourself to three false casts.

There is another good reason to do this. When fishing, there is rarely a need to make more than three or four false casts. If you get into the habit of limiting your false casts on the water, you will be a more effective fly fisher, because your fly will spend less time in the air with the birds and more time in the water with the fishes. When you learn to shoot line in the next chapter, your limit of three false casts will, paradoxically, help you achieve greater distance per cast: The fewer chances you give yourself to move the rod, the more line you will make yourself shoot on each cast to reach your target.

THE LINE HAND DEBUTS

You're about to make a leap here. Start holding the line in your left hand, not pinned against the grip. For obvious reasons, this is now called your *line hand.* Your hands should be separated by 12 to 18 inches and there should be roughly an 18-inch belly of slack hanging between your line hand and the reel. There should be *no* slack between your line hand and the first stripping guide. Make some four-part casts and then some false casts while holding the

Begin to cast with the line in your left hand, not pinned against the grip. Keep the same spacing between your hands throughout the cast.

line in this manner. Be sure to keep the same spacing between your hands throughout the cast; do not separate your hands during the backcast and re-unite them during the forward cast. This will prevent the fly line from sliding up through the guides at the wrong time during the forward cast, which would reduce the cast's success. Practice holding the line through the entire cast. *Do not* let it slide through your fingers (that's for the next chapter). Get accustomed to this—it is what much of real trout fishing is all about.

TIP CASTING

If you need to cast your fly a mere 25 feet to a rising trout, you will need to learn to cast just by flexing the tip of the rod against the short section of fly line in the air. This will feel like just a little flick of the rod tip at the end of the backcast and forward cast. Hold the line in your line hand, not pinned against

What Is the Loop?

When you watch someone else cast, you'll see a bend or loop of line fly off the rod tip after each stop of the backcast, forward cast, and roll cast. This loop is the vehicle for the line's progress. Its unfurling is what straightens the line behind and in front. When you hear someone say, "You throw a nice loop," that is a high compliment. If they say, "You throw a tight loop," you've really arrived. The smaller the distance between the top and bottom of the loop, the tighter the loop is said to be. Other things being equal, the tighter your loop, the better able you will be to cast into the wind and to cast longer distances.

A tight-loop backcast.

A tight-loop forward cast. If you can make tight loops, you'll have a great fly-fishing life.

A wide-loop backcast.

A wide-loop forward cast. A loop like this makes fishing difficult.

the grip. Make the pickup as usual, but make a very short backcast. You'll hardly need to move your forearm at all: you can use your wrist almost exclusively if that's comfortable. Practice these as four-part casts, and then as sets of three false casts. Practice minimalism. Do the least possible to flip the tip (pop the stop) and send the loop of line on its way. Practice doing *too little,* so little that even the 25-foot cast doesn't straighten out in front. Then increase the energy of your stroke so the line and leader just barely unfurl. It will feel as if you are cheating, that casting *can't* require so little energy and motion in the rod.

In a tip cast, move the rod through a very short arc and just barely flip the rod tip. Do the least possible to flip the tip (pop the stop) and send the loop of line on its way. Notice how high the rod points at the stop.

MIDSECTION CASTING

This is what you've been practicing all this time. Hold the line in your line hand, not pinned against the grip. Make three false casts followed by a presentation. If your rod and line are properly matched, a 45-foot cast should load the rod into the midsection, and you'll feel it bending more than it did during the tip cast. You should notice that your arm, hand, and rod have to travel farther to successfully make the cast. *The longer the cast, the farther back the rod must travel during the back cast and the farther forward it must travel during the forward cast.*

A typical 45-foot cast requires that the rod move through a longer arc, bending into its midsection.

The loop from a midsection cast is wider than the loop from a tip cast.

Shadow Casting

Near my house in Maine is a college whose great expanse of playing fields is surrounded by tall pines. Sometimes, when the sun is just peeking over the pines, a fly caster is seen there. Turning himself so the sun illuminates his left side, he false casts, watching to the right his stop positions in shadows on the grass or snow. Unlike the videotape, the shadows show him instantly how he is casting. He likes the simplicity of it, thinking Thoreau would have preferred it this way.

CASTING A REAL FLY

Up until now you've been casting a practice fly made of yarn. A fly with a hook usually weighs more than the yarn. You'd think a heavier fly would be easier to cast than something nearly weightless, but the opposite is true. It is dramatically more difficult to cast a big fly or a "heavy" fly, such as one that incorporates lead to make it sink, than a small, light fly.

In fly casting, the weight of your line needs to be such that it "bosses around" your feather of a fly. If the feather is weighed down, it tends a have a mind of its own as the loop unfurls, and it tends to boss the line around instead. What does this mean to you? *When you first start fishing, use the smallest unweighted fly that is reasonable for the fish you will catch.* Unless you are breezing through the casts in this book, don't tie on a size 8 Woolly Bugger, because it will probably be unruly when you cast and fish it.

If you are after trout or panfish, try using a dry fly such as a size 14 Adams or Royal Wulff. In the next chapter, you'll learn how to animate your fly, and you can start swimming a nymph such as a size 14 Gold-Ribbed Hare's Ear or Pheasant Tail. These flies will get you started safely. As your casting improves, you can move to the larger, weightier flies. (Casting seriously heavy flies is described in Chapter 9.)

Even expert fly rodders cringe when the fish require them to cast heavy flies. Add wind to the mix, and these flies will eventually hit anybody in the vicinity. It feels like getting shot by a BB gun, and it's one reason you should always wear glasses and a hat while fly fishing. I once fished with a guide in breezy Belize who said he often worked in a thick wool sweater (despite the steamy-hot tropical climate). When I asked him why, he replied, simply, "Bad fly casters, mon." His clients weren't necessarily bad casters, but they were fishing weighted flies in windy conditions.

PLAYING AROUND

- **Make 20 or 30 consecutive false casts.** Why not? Live dangerously. Once you have mastered the three-false-cast series, you have a license to practice perpetual false casting. *This is perhaps the single fastest way to* *progress as a caster.* It builds muscle memory faster than the four-part cast, and it tends to expose any casting flaws. Yes, it can lead to bad fishing habits by keeping the fly out of reach of the fish. But it sure feels good, and if the fish have to wait for the fly because you like to cast it back and forth in the air, picturing yourself as the graceful caster in your own fly-fishing movie, so be it.

- **Practice casting tight loops and wide loops.** During your series of 20 or 30 false casts, make your loops as tight as you can, then widen them. To go from tight to wide, lengthen your casting arc—that is, make your rod stops occur farther apart. You can also do this by easing off or softening your pop/stops.

- **Experiment with your casting style.** Now is a good time to play with the elbow lift. Remember in Chapter 2, when you learned that you can elevate your elbow during the backcast? Maybe you chose to adopt that style over the elbow-at-your-side style for short to medium-length casts. Continuous false casting is a great way to try the alternative to see if it suits you. Holding the mark in your line hand, make a few false casts with your elbow relaxed at your side. Then make some with your elbow rising and falling 3 or 4 inches with each casting stroke. Keep doing the one that feels and works best.

- **Make the presentations at random.** This is a fun exercise! Have a friend watch you false cast and periodically say, "Now," during a forward cast. At that time, complete the forward cast as usual with the abrupt stop and the rod pointing at the usual 45 degrees above the horizon. Then make the presentation. This forces you to make every forward cast identical to the preceding one, because you never know when it will be your last. It's a great cure for "last-cast-itis," the disease that makes casters think the last forward cast must be more powerful than the ones that preceded it.

- **Make the fly land before the line.** Trout fishers sometimes use this cast when fishing eddies in fast water. It allows the fly to get the longest possible natural drift in the eddy before the fast water drags the line and fly away. It's also just plain fun. Cast in a vertical plane and stop your backcast nearly straight up. Then make your forward cast a little more powerful than normal and stop the rod a little closer to vertical than normal. Done correctly, this will cause your fly to touch the water just as the leader unfurls. The fly therefore gets to the water before the line has had time to fully descend. It works best with heavier flies or with short, stout leaders and short casts. Again, be patient. This technique is best practiced without presentations, during continuous false casting. Try to make the fly kiss the surface at the end of each forward cast. Later, you'll learn the curve cast, which is this same cast made in a horizontal plane.

TROUBLESHOOTING

Two Common Problems

1. **The line seems to be flying right at your face during the backcast.** Keep the rod tilted off to the side and make sure that you are properly positioned in any crosswind, as you learned in Chapter 2.

2. **It's just not working— your forward cast isn't extending fully.** This usually happens for one of four reasons:

   • You forgot to pop/stop on your forward cast, your backcast, or both.

   • Your backcast stopped progressively farther and farther beyond vertical. It should stop in the same spot every time.

To land the fly first, before the line, make your forward cast a little more powerful than normal and stop the rod a little closer to vertical than normal.

   • You didn't wait for the line to straighten behind you or in front of you before starting your next cast. Make a longer pause before you start the next cast.

   • Your last forward cast is too strong, stronger than the preceding ones. Make every forward cast a clone of the previous one; each one should have the same amount of energy.

CHAPTER 6

Lengthening Your Cast (Stripping + Shooting + False Casting)

Stop here if you have no predatory instincts, because the next technique is going to cause *a lot* of fish to bite your fly. Most fish bite things that move. A little pseudo-animal (your fly) moving through the water looks like lunch to trout, bass, pike, walleye, striped bass, bonefish, tuna, you name it. If you can move your fly through the water for 20 feet and repeatedly cast it back to where you started, you can go almost anywhere on this earth and catch fish. If you can move it through 30 or 40 feet of water, over and over again, hundreds of times a day, you'll be positively dangerous.

So far, you have learned to cast the fly onto the water with the roll cast and the four-part cast, to pick it up, cast it again, and to false cast it. In this chapter, you are going to learn how to animate your fly, to make it come alive, by stripping (pulling) it toward you. This is a critical, but easy, stage in your evolution as a fly fisher. Once you strip line in, you'll need to extend it back out. This is done in the air by allowing line to shoot through the guides after each forward-cast stop. Shooting

Some Words About Distance

It is fun, but not practical, to cast an entire 80- or 90-foot fly line with a fly on the end. It is rarely necessary to cast more than 60 feet. However, being able to do so gives you the tools you need to fish in some pretty difficult conditions. If you want to make casts longer than 50 feet, be sure to use a line with a weight-forward taper. Because of its extra weight and thickness beyond 50 feet, a double taper is not suitable for long casts.

Blue River, Indiana

You are in a kickboat, in stocking-foot waders with fins on your feet, floating the Blue River in southern Indiana. You've heard that people fish here for things like redear sunfish, smallmouth bass, and rock bass. Live crayfish are the bait of choice among local anglers. You are fishing your trusty black Woolly Bugger on your 9-foot 6-weight rod. You are making 50-foot casts to submerged logs and rocks, and to places where the water is a deep green and has cut away the banks beneath the sycamore trees. You are animating the fly back toward your boat with 1-foot strips, bringing it in about 25 feet with each retrieve. Then you make your pickup and three successive false casts, shooting some line with each forward stroke so that the fly extends back to about 50 feet. You do this for hours, shooting line on each false cast and stripping the fly back toward you. Every few minutes a goggle-eyed rock bass, with its oversized red eyes, bites your fly. And if it's not a rock bass, it's a pumpkinseed, with its brilliant orange and blue hues. Occasionally a feisty little smallmouth attacks your fly. The fishing is good and you think about how many waters there are to fish and how you'll never live long enough to fish them all.

Float-tubing is a great way to fish waters too small for a powerboat or too windy for a canoe. Notice that the backcast stop is the same in a float tube as it is when you are standing.

is not difficult; it just takes practice. Along with double-hauling, it will be the great leap forward in your fly fishing.

CLEAN YOUR LINE. NOW!

It is imperative that you have a clean fly line when you learn to shoot. A clean line will run freely through the guides and out toward the fish. A dirty line will drag through the guides and simply won't shoot well. This is just as frustrating for an advanced fly fisher as it is for a novice. At the L.L. Bean Fly-Fishing School, we used to clean the lines every day before we taught shooting. (We now use lines with a coating that all but eliminates the need to clean the line. If your line lacks this technology, you should clean it often.)

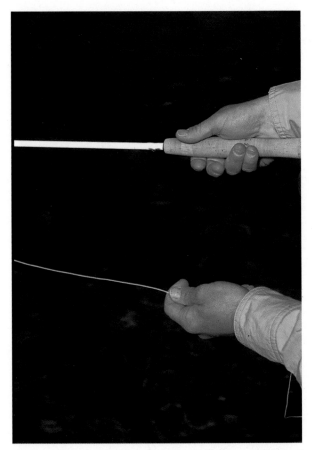

To establish two-point control, bring your line hand directly to your rod hand . . .

ESTABLISH TWO-POINT CONTROL

Start by holding the 37-foot mark in your line hand, with the line straight on the water. Bring your line hand directly to your rod hand and transfer the line to your rod hand. Pin the line loosely against the grip while continuing to hold line with your other hand. This is called two-point control, because you have control of the line with both hands. When you are fishing and the line is on the water, you should *always* have two-point control. This will enable you to retrieve the fly, and to begin to retrieve the fish once you hook it.

When you are about to cast, release the line from the

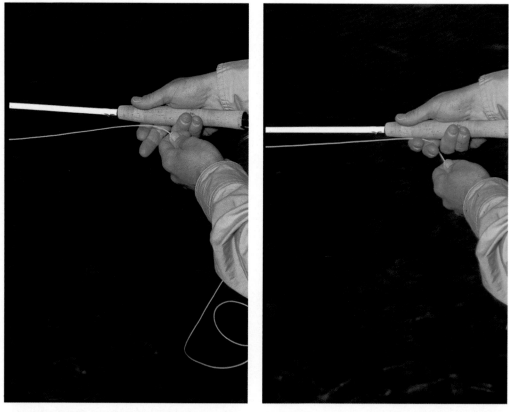

. . . and transfer the line to your rod hand.

This is the hard way to establish two-point control.

You should establish two-point control whenever the line is on the water. It gives you control of the line with both hands.

grip and hold it in your line hand for the cast. *You should not have two-point control during any part of the cast.* Once the cast is back on the water, re-establish two-point control. Yes, this conflicts with what you learned in earlier chapters, but pinning the line against the grip was recommended initially to make learning as easy as possible. Now you'll need to unlearn that technique to cast and fish in the real world.

STRIPPING WITH TWO-POINT CONTROL

Make sure your rod is pointing *down* at the water when you do this. (Many advanced flyfishers actually put the tip in the water while stripping line.) In your practice so far, when you've pinned the line against the grip, you've had a 2-foot length of line hanging down between your rod hand and the reel. Start this sequence from that position.

- Using your line hand, grasp the line hanging just below your rod hand (you now have two-point control) and pull 18 inches of line through the space between the fingers of your rod hand and the grip. (Don't use more than two fingers on your rod hand for this.) Allow the line to slide freely through your rod hand. This is called stripping.

- Drop the 18 inches of line you just stripped with your line hand and pick it up again just below the fingers of your rod hand. Pull another 18 inches of line through the fingers of your rod hand.

- Repeat this over and over again until you have pulled in most of the line.

Again, point your rod *down* at the water when you do this. You can see that if you keep doing this, you will pull any slack out of the line and your fly will "swim" toward you. Stripping with a low rod tip is how a fly should be animated, not by pumping or twitching the rod as a spin fisher would. This is also the best position from which to detect a fish biting a subsurface, out-of-sight fly, and from which to then set the hook.

Practice stripping by pulling the line straight back and away from your line hand versus pulling the line straight down from your rod hand. This will protect the fingers of your rod hand from getting line burns. In saltwater fly fishing, for example, you may strip the fly with fast, 3-foot-long pulls through

Stripping straight down is comfortable for most fishing . . .

. . . but to prevent line burns when stripping fast, pull the line back rather than down from your line hand.

Why Should the Rod Tip Be So Close to the Water?

There's a good casting reason: When you start the pickup with the rod tip by the water, you have more potential distance in which to make a smooth pickup and good backcast. On the other hand, a good trout fishing position when you want your fly to drift naturally ("dead drift") in the current is with the rod up in the air. But this compresses the arc in which the rod can make the pickup and backcast, making those parts of a cast more difficult for a beginner.

Trout fishing from the dead-drift position. With practice, you will be able to make a pickup from this position.

There's a good fishing reason for keeping the tip low: When you are stripping your fly through the water with the rod tip low, there is no slack to diminish your retrieve, so every twitch of your line hand translates directly into the swimming of your fly. Also, when a fish strikes, the absence of slack lets you make the strongest possible hook set, if needed.

Keeping the rod tip low not only helps you achieve a good pickup, but also good fly response to stripping, sensitive strike detection, and solid hook sets.

many hundreds of yards of water in a day. This technique of pulling straight back can help you avoid some real pain. You usually don't make such long or fast strips in trout or bass fishing, so it's less painful to strip down instead of back in those types of fishing.

PREPARING TO SHOOT

- Starting with the mark in your line hand and the line straight on the water, establish two-point control, and strip in 3 feet of line.
- From your line hand, drop the portion you just stripped; then grasp the line again just below the fingers of your rod hand.
- Holding the line in your line hand, release the line from the grip *before* you make the pickup. From now on, *always release the line from the grip before you make a pickup* (thereby releasing two-point control). This will help you immensely with shooting and, eventually, with double hauling (see Chapter 8).

HOW TO SHOOT

Begin your usual four-part cast. The pickup and backcast are unchanged. When shooting, however, the forward cast requires a tiny bit more energy in the pop/stop than usual. (Most casters overpower their casts unknowingly, even when they aren't shooting.) The *instant after* you stop your forward cast, release your hold on the line and let it slide through your fingers and up through the guides. The momentum of the unfurling loop will pull the slack between your line hand and reel out through the guides. The presentation is as always—while the line falls to the water, allow the rod tip to fall with it.

If you started by stripping in 3 feet from your mark, all 3 feet of line should have shot out through the guides. In the beginning, practice shooting line only at the end of the forward cast. Later, as you progress, you'll find that you can also shoot line at the end of the backcast.

Many casters mistakenly try to help the shooting of line by overpowering the forward cast, by moving the rod in a longer arc toward the horizontal, or by trying to push the line up through the guides with their line hand. The only extra things you should do are:

- Use a *slightly* more emphatic pop/stop.
- Release the line the instant after the rod stops on the forward cast.

Where should the rod be pointing after this stop? Right where it has always stopped: at 45 degrees above the horizon.

Practice this sequence many times over. Start at the mark; establish two-point control; strip in 3 feet of line; release the line from the grip; make a pickup, backcast, and forward cast; release the line to shoot; then lower the rod tip to the water as the line falls. Only after you can comfortably shoot the 3 feet of line out to the mark should you progress to False Casting + Shooting.

The instant after you stop your forward cast, release your hold on the line and let it slide through your fingers and up through the guides.

FALSE CASTING + SHOOTING

This is a watershed in your development as a fly fisher, not just as a caster. A four-part cast puts the fly 45 feet away. Stripping in 3 feet and shooting it back out lets you fish the area only from 42 to 45 feet away. Being able to shoot line on three or four successive forward casts will let you extend your fishing beyond 45 feet, and it will let you fish the water within 42 feet. This will open a whole world to you.

Except for certain types of trout fishing, this is the technique that you will use every time you go fly fishing, for the rest of your life. *When combined with stripping, it is the single most important sequence in this book.* When you master

False Casting + Shooting = The Road to Bliss

I was once fishing a small lake in Wyoming that had a well-deserved reputation for large rainbows and cutthroats. There were a few other anglers on the water who, like me, were in float tubes. I was having outstanding fishing with my good old black Woolly Bugger, casting it out 50 feet and retrieving it erratically to within a few feet of the rod tip. In the pellucid mountain water, I could see the fish following it and being antagonized into striking by the long, stuttering retrieve.

The other anglers around me seemed unable to false cast and shoot line, so they couldn't cast the fly back out after such a retrieve. They were either making four-part casts or trolling. They didn't catch much. If they could only have done what you are about to do here, they could have had much better fishing that day.

it, all fly-fishing doors will be open to you—whether you're fishing streamers for trout, poppers for bass, or shrimp imitations for bonefish on the Florida flats.

Make sure the area at your feet is clear of things that can catch the line. A lawn is ideal for this. You are going to make your habitual three false casts, allowing some line to shoot at the end of each forward cast.

- Begin by stripping in 10 feet of line from the mark and allowing it to pile at your feet.

- Make the pickup, and firmly hold the line in your line hand during the backcast and forward cast.

- Immediately *after* the forward-cast stop, release it and allow it to shoot perhaps 2 feet. Pinch it firmly with your line hand just as the leader unfurls at the end of the forward cast.

- Make the second backcast and forward cast, releasing line *after* the second forward-cast stop, to shoot roughly 3 feet.

- Firmly pinch and hold the line through the third backcast and forward cast, shooting the last 3 feet of line *after* the forward cast stop.

- Make your presentation, returning the rod tip to the water.

- Do this many times over until it is comfortable.

You'll notice that your first false cast, with only 20 feet of fly line in the air, may not shoot well. This is because there is less line weight for the rod to load against, so the rod consequently bends and unbends less when you stop. To counteract this, make quicker casting strokes over shorter casting arcs with short lengths of line. Your first one or two strokes should be aggressive tip casts. As the line lengthens with each forward-cast shoot, your stroke must become slightly longer in both time and distance, loading the rod into the midsection.

Like so much of what you learned earlier, this process takes concentration and practice. Your brain must coordinate the pinching and releasing motion of your line hand with your backcast and forward casts. This is a time when you must be patient. Laugh when things go wrong and celebrate when they don't. Once your muscles remember what to do, you'll return to daydreaming as you false cast, shoot, and retrieve your practice fly. As you learned earlier, don't tie on a heavy fly such as a Woolly Bugger or Clouser Minnow. Make sure that you can do this well with a practice fly before you advance to something heavier.

Again, if you have trouble with this sequence, unrig your rod and pantomime it. When you can make this series of casts successfully, you are truly ready to fish the world.

SHOOTING BEYOND 45 FEET

You may be ready now to make longer casts, beyond 45 feet. As the cast lengthens, your stroke must become slightly longer in both time and distance, loading the rod deeper into the midsection. Remember: *The longer your cast, the farther back the rod must travel during the backcast and the farther forward it must travel during the forward cast.* This means your thumbnail will point well beyond vertical at the backcast stop. And, because there is more line to unfurl in the air, your pauses must be longer, too.

- Pull more line off the reel, 10 feet past the 37-foot mark, and let it fall.
- Hold the mark and, with the line straight on the water, make a pickup.
- Make just two false casts, shooting 5 feet of line after each forward-cast stop.

If your line is clean and your casts are true, you should see that extra 10 feet of line shoot out through the guides. That's a 55-foot cast! Do that over and over again.

Up to a point (casting does have limits), the more line you are carrying in the air at the beginning of the cast, the more you can shoot at the end of the cast. You will eventually get to the stage where you'll shoot all of those extra 10 feet in just one forward stroke.

Five Reasons Why You Should Learn to Cast 90 Feet

1. Why else are fly lines so long?
2. It's a good way to lose weight.
3. It'll look great on your resume.
4. Fly casting may someday be an Olympic event.
5. It will enhance your love life.

Videotape: Your Virtual Casting Instructor

You've come this far, patiently reading, studying the photographs, and practicing. You owe it to yourself to see yourself cast. Tape yourself. Other than having a live casting instructor to help you improve, this is the most effective learning tool you can use.

Set up your camera on a tripod and point it perpendicular to your casting direction. It should be on the same side of your body as your rod hand. At first, make sure the lens setting is just wide enough to include the rod on both the forward and backcast. Do a series of four-part casts and false casts. Then set the lens to a wider angle to capture the shape of the loops as they come off the rod tip on both the forward cast and backcast. Repeat the casts you did earlier. When you play the tape of your casting, use the pause button so you can compare your hand, arm, and rod positions to the ones you see in this book. Your forward and backcast loops should be the same size and shape, like mirror images. Finally, cast directly at the camera. On tape, you should see the rod travel in the same plane on the forward and backcasts.

PICKUP FROM THE DEAD-DRIFT POSITION

When fishing your fly dead drift (without dragging it through the water), you'll have your rod tip up in the air when the fly is on the water. It would be tedious to lower your rod tip and pull in slack so you can make the smooth pickup you've learned every time you cast. Instead, practice the pickup and four-part cast beginning from the dead-drift position. Having mastered the smooth pickup from the low-rod position, you'll be surprised by how easy it is to now make both the pickup and backcast in such a short arc of rod, from the dead-drift position.

PLAYING AROUND

- **Shoot line on the roll cast.** Make a roll cast that has a particularly aggressive pop/stop, one that has a tight loop and lots of power. Shoot some line immediately after the stop of the roll cast. You'll get the best results if you do it with the two-handed roll cast you learned earlier. You'll have to shoot line from its pinned-against-the-grip position. This is a good technique to use when you are fishing in front of a high bank or a lot of vegetation. Practice this one, because it's another one that will impress your friends and catch more fish.

- **Shoot line on your forward cast *and* your backcast.** You're skilled enough now to do this, and you already know how. In addition to shooting after the forward-cast stop, do it after your backcast stop, too. It will double the rate at which you pinch and release the line. It may feel awkward at first, but you will get used to it and it will pay off in fewer false

For better shooting from your backcast, pivot the reel to the side.

casts and more time with your fly in the water. (There is a technique that will make line shoot more readily on your backcast—pivot the reel to the side during the backcast. This is unorthodox, but it really works.)

- **Get the most from the least.** Practice shooting as much line as possible on each false cast. Make a 55-foot cast and strip your fly 30 feet toward you. See how few false casts it takes to get the fly back out to 55 feet. This getting-the-most-from-the-least is the path to elegance.

TROUBLESHOOTING

Three Common Problems

1. **The line is hardly shooting through the guides.** Make sure that:
   - your line is clean.
   - your four-part cast is unchanged from what you were doing in earlier chapters.
   - your forward cast pop/stops at the 45-degrees-above-horizontal position.
   - you release the line the instant (one nanosecond) after the forward-cast stop;
   - you put a slightly more emphatic pop/stop at the end of each forward cast.

2. **The line slides through the guides *during* instead of *after* the forward cast and ends up in a heap in front of you.** You'll know this is

By popping the rod too early in the cast, you may cause a tailing loop. This will often tangle your leader.

happening because you can hear your line hissing as it slides through the guides during the forward cast. To cure this, hold the line firmly without slippage until the nanosecond *after the forward cast has stopped.* It may be easier if you first make some four-part casts in which you just hold the line in your line hand without shooting. Once you are confident that you can hold the line during the cast, try releasing it again after the stop. If you still struggle with this, that's okay. It happens to a lot of casters. Put the rod down and pantomime, in slow motion, the entire cast. Be sure to hold the imaginary line firmly until just after the rod has stopped.

3. **The last forward cast is getting tangled on itself.** This is called a tailing loop. It occurs when the pop is made in the beginning or middle of the forward cast instead of immediately before the stop. It causes the rod tip to dip low, then spring back up, and that's what fouls up the line. Many casters do it by making the last in a series of false casts different in style than the previous casts: they try to pop the cast too early in the stroke, long before the stop. One sneaky way to fix this is: *Just don't make the last cast!* Instead, present the fly on your second-to-last cast. This will cause you to make the last stroke just like the previous ones, albeit with the wee bit more energy you add on each successive forward stroke. Remember, no matter how long or energetic your cast, the pop must occur at the very end of your casting stroke, immediately before the stop.

Tailing loops often cause wind knots to form in your leader. They significantly weaken your leader and should be cut out.

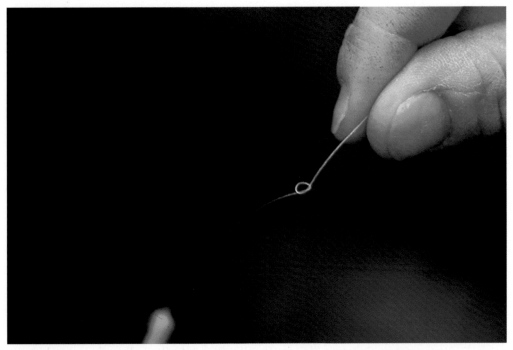

A wind knot, usually in the tippet, often results from a tailing loop. This one has not yet tightened.

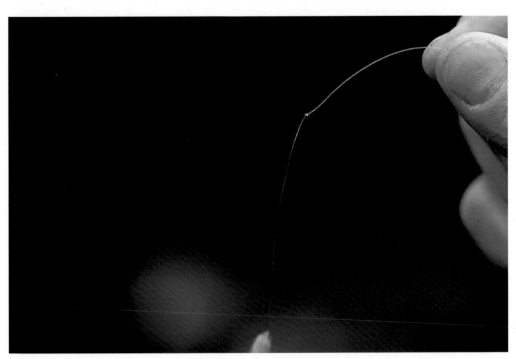

This is a tightened wind knot, which will weaken the leader dramatically. It should be cut out and the fly re-tied.

CHAPTER
7

Wind Casting

W e may as well get used to it: wind is nature's way of distributing heat around the globe. Much of this activity seems to happen in places that have great fly fishing—places like western Montana, with its wealth of rainbows and indigenous cutthroats; southern Chile, with its huge European brown trout; the Florida Keys, with their silver-bullet bonefish. With practice and patience, you may be able to fly cast successfully in 20-mph winds. It's not easy, but it will keep you on the water after others have gone home. In this chapter you'll learn skills to let you fish in some pretty difficult conditions.

CASTING IN CROSSWINDS

These are the easiest to cope with. A crosswind from your left side enables you to use the standard four-part cast, roll cast, or false cast on your right side. If the wind is particularly strong, cast in a sidearm plane. This is just a fly cast tilted completely on its side with the rod moving in a horizontal plane throughout the cast. Be careful to keep your tight casting arc and to use your usual disciplined stop positions.

Beartooth Plateau, Southwestern Montana

You are standing on the shore of an unnamed lake 10,000 feet high on Montana's Beartooth Plateau. It is stormy. The wind is howling down the lake, right into your face, bringing all the fish food from the surface with it. There are 15-inch brook trout that have never seen a fly before, feeding indiscriminately just a few rod lengths out. The wind is pushing you away from the water. The experts would say that your leader is too short and stubby for your size 10 black Woolly Bugger, but it's too much trouble to add tippet right now. You make a vertical backcast and drive your forward cast down hard to the water. Your fly slams the surface and a brookie smashes it instantly. You set the hook and silently scoff at the leader mavens. It's a nice fish. You are no longer mad at the weather.

A sidearm cast is helpful in crosswinds. Tilt the rod nearly to the horizon.

During the sidearm cast, keep your casting arc small to make your loops tight.

If the wind is coming from your right side, do what you did earlier in the off-shoulder roll cast. Tilt the rod over your head so the tiptop travels on your downwind side. Push your elbow slightly out to the side and bring your hand in close so your hand and forearm point to the top of your head. This keeps your hand on your right side, where it is strongest, and puts the rod tip over your left shoulder. The wind will now blow the line away from you instead of into you. Otherwise, the cast itself is done exactly as you did it before. Most important is to keep the rod moving in the same plane forward and backward, not in a curving motion.

If the crosswind from the right is gentle, a sidearm cast may work for you, although I still prefer the off-shoulder under these conditions.

Why not cast left-handed if there's a crosswind from the right? This may sound appealing, but the fact is that fishing with your off hand will feel as if you are trapped in someone else's body. The casting itself doesn't feel so odd—you practiced it earlier—but stripping your fly and setting the hook feel, well, strange. And when you actually hook a fish, you'll want to put the rod back into your dominant hand anyway. But try it. You may like it.

If the wind is coming from your rod side, cast off-shoulder and the wind will blow the line and fly to your downwind side.

CASTING INTO A HEADWIND

The most effective way to make short to medium-length casts into a headwind is keep your loop tight. Keep the length of your casting arc and of your pop/stop as short as possible. Yes, this limits your distance, but you're up against what lawyers call an act of God, so relax. The more you grit your teeth and try to punch the cast into the wind, the more trouble you'll have. This often causes tailing loops and the resulting wind knots. No, wind doesn't cause the knots, but it can induce you to make the tailing-loop error that causes them.

Another strategy in a headwind is to make a sidearm cast. Because wind speed is slowest just above the ground (or water), this lets you cast your line underneath the strongest winds.

You can also make your backcast more vertical and your forward cast farther down than usual. Casting forward and downward makes the line straighten when the fly is just inches, instead of feet, above the water, so it won't be blown back at you.

If you need to make longer casts into the wind, learn to double haul, as shown in the next chapter.

The Roll Cast Pickup

Sometimes it can be awkward to make a straight-line, low-rod-tip pickup. This can occur when there's a tailwind. It happens more commonly when you're fishing dead drift (rod tip up) upstream, and your fly has drifted back close to your position. (There is often a lot of slack on the water when the fly has drifted close to you.) You've practiced making a pickup from this position, but it can be difficult to do well with all that slack. Instead, try something else: a roll-cast pickup. Your high rod-tip position requires you to move the tip back only a few feet into your setup position. Make the usual forward-stroke portion of the roll cast. After the line has fully extended in the air, but before it has hit the water, make a backcast. You have just substituted a roll cast for a conventional pickup. This may seem inconsequential, but you'll find more and more situations in which to apply it. It is another one of those casts that is inexplicably satisfying.

CASTING WITH A TAILWIND

If you're using a floating line and you don't need lots of distance, make a roll cast. A tailwind can really boost the power of this cast, and can make an anemic roll cast look as if it's on steroids. If the tailwind is strong, you may have some difficulty with your setup, because the wind may keep blowing it forward. Try setting up with your rod tilted farther back toward the rear than usual.

You can also make a more downward backcast and a

In a strong headwind, you can make a nearly vertical backcast . . .

. . . and a slightly more emphatic, more downward forward cast than usual.

more upward forward cast than usual. This keeps the backcast a bit lower, under the strongest winds, than it would normally be. The forward cast is then lofted upward, where it is caught by the wind and sailed out over the water. Also try the sidearm backcast. This keeps the backcast close to the ground, where the wind is slowest. You can then violate the rules and allow your forward cast to swing upward somewhat, lofting the line up into the carrying winds.

FISH YOUR BACKCAST

Face backwards, into the wind, and make a forward cast into the wind. Once the forward cast has unfurled, turn and direct your forward cast toward the fish. The wind should then help your backcast extend fully. As the backcast falls toward the water, turn around and fish the cast. Because it is easier for most of us to make a tight-loop forward cast than backcast, you'll have a better chance of fully extending the line into the wind with this technique. This may sound like some kind of trick, but saltwater anglers frequently use it when fishing from a boat in windy conditions. You can also use it when your backcast must be carefully placed to avoid snagging in the trees: make a forward cast into a space in the trees, then turn around and fish the backcast.

In a strong tailwind, fish your backcast; make the forward cast into the wind.

As the backcast falls, turn around.

Fish your backcast.

Why Few Instructors Can Deliberately Cast Tailing Loops

I serve on a board at the Federation of Fly Fishers that trains and certifies fly-casting instructors. One of the requirements for certification is that instructors be able to make all the "bad" casts—from wide open loops to tailing loops. To be effective, good instructors must be able to demonstrate to their students what they are doing wrong, requiring the instructor to make the same kind of faulty cast that the student is making. An inability to cast a tailing loop on demand is probably the biggest stumbling block for prospective instructors. Why? Because they have to override their muscle memory of the good cast. So, how do they learn to throw bad casts? The same way they established their muscle memory. Practice.

PLAYING AROUND

Don't play around when it's windy or you will displease the fish gods. If you insist, try this drill, but only when it's calm. It is a fascinating mind/body game to play.

Deliberately Cast Tailing Loops

Having spent all this time willing your body to do the right thing, you are now going to teach it to do the wrong thing. Sounds crazy? Yep, this is another one of those counterintuitive ideas that works. Like careening Dad's car around an icy vacant parking lot, it's a great way to learn how *not* to do something. Learning to deliberately cast tailing loops makes you much less likely to throw them accidentally when it's windy, when they most often occur.

Start by making some of your usual false casts. Now, make some in which you pop the forward cast too early. Pop long before you stop. In other words, make the burst of acceleration come at the beginning or in the middle of the cast instead of at the end. If you see tailing loops, you win! Just don't make a habit of this.

TROUBLESHOOTING

Expect occasional wreckage when it's windy. You may cast tailing loops and wind knots, you may get hit by the fly or stung by the line, you may end up with your line tangled in a macramé project. As always, be patient. The more train wrecks you have, the more you will learn how to avoid them. If you're like me, you'll suffer through the lesson many, many times before you get it right. Yes, fly fishing is hard work, but you're just the right person for the job.

CHAPTER 8

The Double Haul

If you are coordinated enough to ride a bicycle or drive a car, you can learn to double haul. When you do, your overall fishing success will make a quantum leap. The double haul turbocharges your fly cast by increasing the speed at which the loop travels and unrolls. It turns *less* into *more*. It actually lets you cast a tighter loop and a faster line, over more distance, all while doing less work with your rod hand. Simply put, it makes your fly get out there faster and makes long casts less work and more fun. And I mean fun!

Done correctly, a double haul is nearly as exciting as that first time you rode your bike without training wheels. Most double-haulers can tell you exactly when and where they first learned to do it.

This technique requires the line hand to tug on the line during the forward cast and again during the back-

Turneffe Atoll, Belize, Central America

On the second-largest barrier reef in the world, you are wading an immense expanse of coral sand and marl that teems with tiny crabs, grass shrimp, and other bonefish foods. The wind is blowing, as it almost always does in the tropics. You are using a 9-foot 8-weight rod with a 12-foot 0X leader. Your fly is a size 6 Crazy Charlie, and it looks like some cheap piece of costume jewelry. Even at high tide the water is rarely more than 4 feet deep. Any fish you hook here has only one place to go—away—and only one speed at which to swim—Mach 1. Your guide sees a school of dozens of 3-pound bonefish feeding together, with their dorsal fins exposed like silvery sickles glinting in the sun. The bonefish are 80 feet away, swimming toward you in 8 inches of water, and they are hyper-wary of barracuda and good fly casters. Your guide tells you to cast 10 feet in front of them. You double haul, making a couple of false casts off to the side of the school to avoid spooking them. You redirect your last cast in front of the school and your fly drops 60 feet away. The fish are now at 70 feet and closing. They keep coming. Your guide says, "Strip it," and you retrieve the fly 18 inches. A fish breaks for your fly and your guide quietly says, "He's coming." Your heart starts to hammer. Then . . . the alarm rings, you wake up, you smell coffee.

cast, repositioning itself between each cast in preparation for the next one. The tug is called a single haul. The resetting or rebounding of the hand makes it a double haul. When fishing, the double haul is usually combined with shooting to lengthen the cast. Proper double hauling looks exactly like the casting you've done up to this point, with the addition of a well-timed haul and rebound of the line hand.

Even if you only trout fish with dry flies within 45 feet, you should learn this cast. No, it probably won't help you in this kind of fishing. It just feels good! Synchronizing the tug on the line with the stroke of the rod, and feeling the resulting synergy, is perhaps the greatest pleasure in casting.

The double haul is mostly used when:

- casting longer distances, beyond 45 or 50 feet;
- fishing with rods heavier than 6-weights;
- casting into a headwind;
- showing off.

GETTING STARTED

Pull 10 feet of line off the reel past the 37-foot mark and stretch it out at your feet. *Clean the line* (this is essential). Holding the line at the mark, warm up with an easy series of three false casts. Good. Now, put the rod down, because you are going to learn this by pantomiming.

PANTOMIME THE DOUBLE HAUL WITH YOUR HANDS

Carefully do this step by step, in *very* slow motion at first:

1. Start with your rod hand in the forward-cast stop position, with your elbow down, forearm at a right angle to your upper arm, and the imaginary rod pointed up at 45 degrees.
2. Position your line hand just 2 inches below your rod hand. This is the position from which you'll start the double haul.
3. Pantomime your usual backcast. *During* the backcast, pull your line hand and imaginary line directly down and away from your rod hand, so that your hands are separated by approximately 2 feet at the end of the backcast. You just made a single haul.
4. The haul begins slowly as the stroke begins slowly, it accelerates as the rod accelerates, it pop/stops as the rod pop/stops.

In slow motion, pantomime the double haul without a rod. This is your start position for the backcast double haul.

As the rod hand backcasts, the line hand hauls. This is a single haul.

5. Pause for the backcast to unfurl. Freeze your rod exactly as you usually do during the pause. With your rod motionless, bring your line hand back to meet your rod hand, again with the 2 inches of separation. This is a new position for your line hand, with your left arm crossing in front of you.

6. After the pause, pantomime your usual forward cast. As you do, tug your line hand directly away from your rod hand, so there is again about 2 feet of separation. The timing of your haul coincides exactly with the timing of your forward stroke—you are simply accelerating the separation of your hands.

7. As you did after the backcast stop, freeze the rod in the forward-cast stop position and bring your line hand up to within 2 inches of your motionless rod hand.

8. You have just pantomimed a backcast double haul and a forward-cast double haul.

9. Repeat this sequence until you turn blue.

You should do this pantomime dozens of times until the rebounding of your line hand during the rod pauses is a simple reflex action, a down-up motion. As you gradually speed up to a real-time pantomime, you'll see that this

With the rod hand frozen in place, the line hand returns to the rod hand to prepare for the forward-cast haul.

As the rod hand makes the forward cast, the line hand hauls.

As the imaginary forward cast unfurls, the line hand resets to permit the next backcast haul.

The Hardest Parts of the Double Haul

For most people there are three challenges in the double haul. You must:

- Make the line hand bounce back up to meet the rod hand.
- Make sure the rod hand *stays still* while the line hand comes to meet it. (Only very advanced casters can cheat on this one.)
- Tug with the line hand *during* instead of slightly before or after the forward and backcasts. Try to haul *against* the bending of the rod.

rebounding must happen the instant the line hand reaches the bottom of its travel.

PANTOMIME THE DOUBLE HAUL WITH YOUR UNRIGGED ROD

Once you are confident that your pantomime is correct, pick up your unrigged rod and pantomime with that. Use your normal casting stroke with your usual amount of energy. Practice this continuously until:

- Your rod hand moves exactly as it would during false casting with a line.
- Your line hand pulls at the same time your rod hand casts.

Try pantomiming the double haul with an unrigged rod. This is the start position for your backcast double haul.

As the rod hand backcasts, the line hand hauls.

With the rod hand frozen in place, the line hand has returned to the rod hand to prepare for the forward-cast haul.

The rod hand makes the forward cast as the line hand hauls.

The hand has reset to permit a haul on the next backcast.

- Your line hand rebounds instantly after the haul, and the rod hand freezes the rod as it does so.

THE DOUBLE HAUL WITH YOUR RIGGED ROD

- Warm up by holding the line at the mark and making repetitive false casts without shooting.

Just keep the line pinched in your line hand for now.

- Keeping the line pinched (don't shoot yet), start double hauling. Feel the extra bend in your rod as your haul against it. Your hauls should be timed

> ### Timing and Length of the Haul
>
> The easiest way to haul is to do it throughout the casting stroke. The speed of the haul should be synchronized with the speed of the cast. That is, the haul begins slowly as the stroke begins slowly, it accelerates as the rod accelerates, it pop/stops as the rod pop/stops.
>
> The length of the haul varies with the length of the casting stroke. As you remember, to cast a longish line—say, 55 feet—you need to move your arm through a longish stroke. Your haul will be correspondingly longer on the 55-foot cast than it is on the preceding 47-foot cast.

The backcast begins.

The line hand hauls during and in opposition to the backcast.

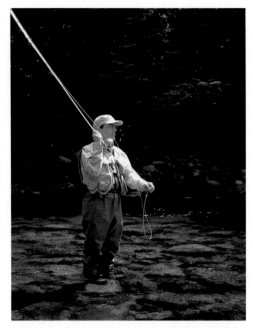

This is a backcast with a single haul. The line hand must now reset to prepare for a haul on the next forward cast.

The line hand resets to the motionless rod hand, enabling a haul on the forward cast.

so that it feels as if you are pulling the line *against* the bend of the rod. (You are.)

- *Don't change your casting stroke at all.*

- During each pause, you should feel the line being pulled up through the guides (it's technically *shooting*) as your line hand rebounds the 2 feet or so to your rod hand. If you are impatient to see results, let the line shoot after one of your forward stops.

To make the line shoot better behind you, swing the reel off to the side during the backcast, as you did when you first learned to shoot. If this seems to foul you up instead, forget that you ever heard of it.

As the rod begins the forward cast, the line hand begins to haul.

The forward cast and forward haul have stopped at the same instant.

The line hand resets, as it does on every double haul.

HAULING AND SHOOTING IN THE REAL WORLD

Practice continuous no-shoot double hauling while false casting: It's a great way to become proficient with the double haul.

- Once you are comfortable with this and you think it's going well, release (shoot) line on the last of your forward false casts. During real fishing, double hauling is usually done in conjunction with shooting.
- You'll know you've made a huge step when you can make a pickup, double haul and shoot some line on the backcast, then double haul and shoot again on the forward cast.
- One test of mastery is that you will make a series of two or three false casts during which you double haul and shoot on every backcast and forward cast. That's what much of real-world tarpon fishing and bonefishing is like.

MELTDOWN

Be prepared for plenty of wreckage and mental meltdown. *It's common to crash and burn a lot as you learn this. Stay with it.* You have to make your brain con-

Videotape Your Double Haul

You'll be amazed by how much you can learn from this. This time, the camera should be on the rod-hand side of your body, slightly forward of perpendicular to your casting direction. This will let you view both the line hand and rod hand together. Watch the tape for any signs that you are doing something other than what you've read. In particular, look for these no-no's:

- Your rod hand comes forward to meet your line hand after the backcast stop. This is called *creep,* and only very advanced casters can get away with it.

- You are not hauling simultaneously with your casting stroke.

- Your forward-cast haul looks like it's only about 3 inches long relative to your rod hand.

This caster couldn't freeze his rod at the backcast while he reset his line hand. Instead, he has brought his rod hand forward to meet his line hand. With so little arc in which to make a forward cast and a forward haul, this cast is doomed.

quer your body's natural impulses. You *will* be successful: Follow these instructions carefully, don't get discouraged, and you will be double hauling soon. I promise.

When you foul up, go back to each step of the instructions and make sure you understand it.

IF ALL ELSE FAILS

- Return to the pantomime and *close your eyes.*
- Move through each step, first with just your hands, then with the un-rigged rod.

Most important, videotape yourself if it's not working, compare the tape to the instructions, and you'll see your error. There may be more than one error, but that does not make you a klutz, just a caster.

PLAYING AROUND

- **Try double hauling with your other hand.** You're pretty hot stuff, being the only person on your block who knows how to double haul. Now it's time for an ego check. Try casting with your left hand and hauling with your right hand. As usual, when you first try it, be ready to laugh at yourself. It is really fun and feels like some strange out-of-body experience. It will definitely make you smile, win friends and influence people. It will probably amuse a few fish, too. But stay with it. Practice! You can do this!

- **Double haul with your eyes closed.** This is another one of those New-Age techniques that really works. It is a great way to concentrate only on the task at hand, and makes you focus on the nuances (we won't call them faults) of your double hauling.
- **Double haul with your leg!** If this guy can do it with his leg, you can do it with your arm.

TROUBLESHOOTING

The best way to troubleshoot is to videotape yourself and compare what you see on the tape to what you see in these instructions and photographs. It will be worth it.

Try hauling with your leg! Here, the leg is reset for the next forward-cast haul. Don't try this after a couple of beers.

CHAPTER
9

Long Casts, Aerial Mends, Special Casts

LONG CASTS

Don't forget to clean, dress, and stretch your line and leader before questing for the far horizon.

The Butt Cast

So far, you've shot casts to about 55 feet with nothing more than the midsection cast, where you made the rod bend into its middle. With the double haul, you added perhaps 10 or 15 feet. An elegant caster can use exactly the same motion that you have been using throughout this book to cast out to 80 feet. But it's easier to do it if you start raising your elbow during the backcast *and* moving the rod through a longer arc. Your stop positions must move farther apart as you make the long cast, and your pauses must be longer. On extremely long casts your backcast and forward stops may be nearly parallel to the ground!

A very long cast requires that the rod bend down into its butt. During the forward cast, try to pull the rod down as you accelerate. Imagine that you are pulling down with your elbow. Here, the pop/stop becomes more of a pull/stop. That is, the motion just before the stop takes longer than a "pop." It's because of the weight of that long line you have suspended in the air. Your little graphite rod doesn't have enough stiffness to let you simply "pop" the tip of the rod to a stop.

When attempting long casts, it may help to hold the trailing end of the grip (just ahead of the reel) and, during the backcast, to swing the reel off to the side. If these things seem to make casting harder, however, don't do them.

Used for very long casts, the butt cast bends the rod nearly to the handle.

Carry a Long Line

This drill is used by the top distance casters in the world, but it works for everybody. What is the longest cast you can make without shooting or double hauling? At that length, pin the line against the grip, then false cast continuously for many repetitions, trying to make a smooth stroke ended by an acceleration/stop. Use the butt cast. Do this until you think you've mastered it. Now let out one more foot of line, pin it, and repeat the drill. Remember that the more line you cast, the longer your casting stroke is and the farther your hand, forearm, and elbow must travel. It may take you quite a while before you are ready to lengthen again, but that's okay. This is a very effective exercise, but only if you are patient.

Add the Double Haul

Once you become comfortable carrying a long line using the method I've described, add the double haul. This may seem simplistic, but it's no less than what the best casters in the world do to cast farther.

The more line you carry, the longer your casting stroke is and the farther your hand, forearm, and elbow must travel.

Once you're comfortable carrying a long line, add the double haul.

AERIAL MENDS

These are used mostly when trout fishing. By placing slack line upstream, you enable the fly to drift farther downstream before the current tightens the line and unnaturally drags the fly. The placing of slack line upstream of the fly before the line hits the water is called an aerial mend. The reach cast is just one of many aerial mends, but it is the easiest and most common.

Reach Cast

In Chapter 6 you learned why the low rod tip is such a good position for animating your fly, setting the hook, and ensuring a smooth pickup. You also learned that, when dead drifting a fly, you should fish with the rod tip elevated. You'll get an even longer dead drift if you make a reach cast. This is a slack-line cast that positions slack fly line upstream of the fly.

To make a reach cast, make a conventional forward cast . . .

. . . and reach upstream with the rod instead of making your usual presentation.

Another view of the reach cast. Stop the forward cast . . .

. . . and reach upstream.

Your upstream reach should be completed before the line lands.

To make a reach cast, do the first three parts of the usual four-part cast. Immediately after the forward cast stop, point the rod about 45 degrees upstream of your stop position and reach upstream with your rod hand as you do. Do this as the line is beginning to fall toward the water. *You need to complete the reach before the line lands.* Otherwise, the movement of the rod upstream will drag the line across the water, which will drag the fly.

The reach cast is virtually the same whether the current flows left-to-right or right-to-left. If it is flowing left-to-right, the reach is simply made across your body. If you are facing directly across the river, for example, your rod should finish the reach cast facing 45 degrees upstream.

Shoot Line During the Reach

Try it; it's just like shooting line at any other time except you are reaching the rod to one side as you do.

S-Cast

The S-cast is another aerial mend, used mainly when you are fishing downstream to selective trout. Immediately after your forward stop, move the rod tip from side to side in tight oscillations. This will cause S's to form in your line as it falls onto the water. The slack S's enable a longer dead drift before the current straightens the line and drags the fly. It is a fun cast with a pretty result.

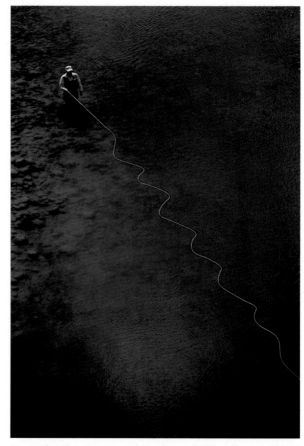

Curve Cast

There are two purposes for a curve cast: first, you want to cast around a corner; second, you want to make an aerial mend by casting some slack upstream of the fly. When I learned the first version, it looked like another magic trick. The idea is to use a sidearm cast with an over-powered forward cast that is

To make the S-cast, move the rod tip side-to-side in tight oscillations just after the forward stop.

then stopped too short. It causes the fly to curve around to the left of the line and is called a positive curve cast.

The fly can be made to lay out to the *right* of the line by underpowering the sidearm cast so that the line falls to the water with the loop intact. This is sometimes called a negative curve. Properly executed, the curve cast literally casts the fly around a corner.

However, unlike the other casts in this book, it is extraordinarily difficult to present a curve cast accurately on the first cast. On the lawn, nailing the latter two out of three practice casts is fine, but not on the water. In my years as a bassaholic, the curve cast has probably landed me a couple of fish that I wouldn't have otherwise caught.

Despite the above disclaimer, this cast is really fun to practice. You'll have an easier time if you practice with a relatively heavy fly and a 7½-foot stout leader and make short casts. Make a sidearm stroke so the loop travels in a horizontal

To curve the line, overpower your sidearm cast, stopping the forward stroke prematurely.

plane, overpower the forward stroke, and stop the forward cast just a little sooner than you normally would. You may recognize this as just a sidearm version of the fly-first cast in Chapter 5.

Anglers for selective trout use the curve frequently to lengthen the dead drift of their flies. They're often willing to sacrifice accuracy for a long, natural drift. Because of the nature of dead-drift fishing, the slack-line version is usually done with a small fly and a long, thin leader. You simply can't make this curve as much as you can with a heavy fly and short, stout leader. You are fighting physics, so don't be disheartened when you encounter this. With practice you can get your cast to curve some, and that's a good outcome.

SPECIAL CASTS

Some of these, such as casting heavy flies and fishing your backcast, are quite practical. Skip casting is sometimes handy to have in your arsenal. Sky casting is whimsical. Hand casting is the ultimate trick cast. If you can hand-cast (see p. 116), you're *good*.

Casting Heavy Flies or Split-Shot

This requires what looks like bad casting technique. You'll have to trust me on this. When casting heavy flies or a leader burdened with split-shot and a strike indicator, you should cast a *wide* loop. You know how to do this: use a longer, slower stroke than usual. Your backcast should tip farther back than usual, and your forward cast should lean farther forward. End with an anemic

When casting heavy flies, make a wide, lethargic loop. Use a longer, slower stroke than usual.

pop/stop or even a SLOP/stop. Imagine that you've taken Valium and you've got the *slows*. That's how to cast weight.

Don't try to make long casts with heavily weighted flies unless you are using a specialized shooting-head line. If you want to learn why, (make sure you are wearing a protective hat and glasses before you do this), pinch two pieces of split-shot right above your practice fly. Then try to make a long cast or some tight loops. It's a disaster, isn't it? You'll never do *that* again. Shorten up your line and try it again with the slow, sleepy, Valium cast. That's the way to do it.

Double hauling works with heavy flies but, again, slow down and lengthen your stroke. Remember the **Playing Around** drill in Chapter 5 (False Casting), when you tried to cast with so little energy that the loop barely got out there? In that drill you used a tight-loop, tip cast. This time, use a slow butt cast. Try that same approach when casting weight. Try to cast *too* slowly, *too* lethargically, and your cast should turn out just right.

Fishing Your Backcast

You did this earlier, when fishing with a tailwind. When you are fishing in a wooded area with some gaps in the trees, turn around and make a forward cast into one of the gaps. Then allow your backcast to simply fall onto the water. Of course, you can just use the roll cast if there are no gaps, but that can limit your distance.

Skip Casting

While practicing the curve cast, try to make the fly skip off the water (it won't work on land) during the forward cast. It's easier to make it skip if you double haul while making continuous false casts, using a sidearm cast. Together, this may sound like a lot, but you know all these techniques. At the beginning of the forward stroke, dip the rod down *slightly*. As the cast progresses, tip the

To skip cast, make a sidearm stroke. Dip the rod tip down slightly during the beginning of the stroke and up slightly as the cast progresses.

rod up slightly. This makes the fly kiss the water on each forward cast. This dipping/tipping is very subtle. Success comes after lots of practice.

What earthly reason would prompt anyone to do this? Some of the world's great trout, bass, and snook fishing lies beneath overhanging vegetation, where a conventional fly cast would land your fly in the trees. While the skip cast is inaccurate and prone to blow up, it's a blast when you skip the fly under some greenery and a fish nails it!

Sky Casting

This is just what it sounds like. It has no real practical application, but it feels good. Like the skip cast, it's easiest to do a sky cast while making continuous false casts with double hauls. Just direct your backcast down into the grass behind you, and the forward cast way up in the air in front of you. This will require your forward cast to stop about 15 degrees short of vertical. You'll be surprised by how high you can launch the practice fly. Don't be surprised if you cast some tailing loops while doing this, because you will have a tendency to move the rod tip in a concave path during the forward stroke. Don't do this if there are rocks behind you, or you'll thrash your line and lose your fly!

Hand Casting

You may have heard about or seen some casting guru casting a fly line with only his or her bare hands. Well, it's surprisingly easy to do this. Why should you try it? Because it's another one of those casts that's just fun to do! Hand casting is also a fine way to improve the timing of your double haul. It can be practiced on land or water but is easier on land. Here's how it goes:

- Use a weight-forward line, not a double taper.
- You *must* clean and lubricate your line. Otherwise, you will burn the skin right off your fingers.
- To reduce drag, make your practice fly no larger than a pea and use either a Nail Knot or a Super Glue connection, not a Loop-to-Loop, for your leader-to-line junction. Both are illustrated in the *L.L. Bean Fly-Fishing Handbook* (The Lyons Press, 1996).
- Start with about 35 feet of line out straight in front of you and some slack at your feet.
- Stand with your left foot well in front of your right foot.

- Lean forward, toward the line. Grasp the line as though you are going to double haul. (You are.)

- Pull the line for the pickup, then accelerate into the backcast. Haul while doing this, just as you would if you were using a rod.
- As you accelerate the haul with your line hand, thrust your rod hand back, pivoting your body to face backwards. *Your elbow should brush right past your ribs* and the backcast should fly past them shortly thereafter. (*The closer you keep your rod hand and elbow to your body, the easier this cast is.*)

- Rebound your line hand to your rod hand as soon as you have finished the haul.

- At this point you should be facing behind you, with most of your weight on your right foot, your rod hand pointing straight back, and your line hand in position to make the forward haul.

- You *must* let the line land on the ground behind you. Trust me.

- Now, simply reverse the sequence for the forward cast. While hauling, bring your rod hand right past your ribs and forward as if you were shov-

ing a sword at the fish. As with the backcast, start slowly and accelerate to a stop. Then let her fly.

The faster and farther apart your hands move during the backcast and forward cast, the longer your hand cast will be. This means that your hauls will seem almost violent compared to the sedate hauls you've made while using a rod.

AFTERWORD

Just One More Cast

If you happen down a certain backroad in Freeport, Maine, on a warm summer evening, you may see something wonderful. The Fly-Fishing School students have left for the day, and now the casting instructors are at play. We are in the company of those who taught before us on that same lawn and casting pool, and of those who taught them. We remember our teachers as we cast: "Joan taught me this way." "Mel teaches it this way." "Lefty describes it this way." We are infatuated with loops of line in the air, with the talk of it, with the teaching of it.

Ellen and Brian are trying out a new technique for teaching the roll cast. Harvey and Joe are going smallmouth bass fishing next week, and they are humorously discussing the best way to cast a big bass bug. For the sheer fun of it, Craig and I are sky casting. After teaching casts for 14 years, Pat is on the casting pool, quietly making four-part casts: pickup, back-cast, forward cast, presentation. Time and again they are beautiful, elegant casts, yet perfection eludes him, as it does all of us. But on this soft summer evening, he moves a little closer.

Index